Symbols of Church Seasons & Days

John Bradner

Symbols of Church Seasons & Days

illustrated by

Betty Wolfe

&

Kerry Dexter

Morehouse-Barlow Company
Wilton, Connecticut

Copyright © 1977 by
Morehouse-Barlow Co., Inc.
78 Danbury Road
Wilton, Connecticut 06897

ISBN 0-8192-1228-8

Library of Congress Card No. 77-70805

Printed in the United States of America

Contents

Foreword

A symbol is intended to suggest meaning. It represents something below the surface. Like a sign it is a means of communication, a device to direct our thinking. Symbolism is a language that may at times remind us of Egyptian hieroglyphics. But all symbolism is not pictorial. Some of it is found in names and phrases, and, in fact, many pictorial symbols had their origin in literature. A great deal of Christian symbolism goes back to the Bible and other writings of many centuries ago. Knowing the background of a symbol enables us to understand the reasons for its use. This is helpful in enjoying art and literature and in using symbolism in our own creative efforts.

The accompanying collection of symbols is arranged according to the chief festivals and seasons of the Christian Year. Items within each season are placed alphabetically. Inevitably there has to be some duplication and overlapping, but the arrangement by season will aid in selecting symbols for creative projects. An index will help users of the book when doing reference work.

The symbols chosen were selected not only from art and decoration but also from names and phrases found in seasonal hymns, legends and Bible passages. An effort has been made to include a number of items not always given in the shorter books of symbols.

Further help in the form of illustration and background may be desired. The author has found most useful two standard works on symbolism: George Ferguson's *Signs and Symbols in Christian Art* and F. R. Webster's *Church Symbolism*. In addition, a dictionary of the Bible and commentaries on individual books of the Bible may be consulted. Pictures and art pamphlets are usually on sale at art galleries and museums. For further suggestions see the bibliography and the appendix of this book.

Note on Bible Versions

Unless otherwise noted, Bible quotations are taken from the Revised Standard Version. In certain cases it is necessary to cite an older translation to bring out the meaning of the symbol being discussed. When this happens, the particular version used will be noted.

Advent

A new Christian year begins with the sesaon of Advent, which starts on the Sunday nearest to November 30th. The first of the four Sundays of Advent is the Church's New Year's Day.

This season of preparation for the celebration of Christmas takes its name from the Latin word which means "coming" and refers to the coming of Christ. Church tradition has assigned two themes to this coming: the first coming, when Jesus Christ was born on Christmas Day, and the second coming at the end of the world when he will return in judgment. Thus the season mixes joy in the redemption that has already come with the sober awe of the judgment which confronts us. Modern interpretation makes Advent a time of spiritual preparation, adding that Christ still is coming—coming into our hearts by grace to redeem and judge us now. He comes in Word and Sacrament, especially in the Holy Eucharist.

Originally Advent was a season of penitential preparation for baptism, but since the sixth century it has been the time of liturgical preparation for Christmas. Although the penitential character has endured, Advent is primarily a season of solemn joy and of anticipation. The traditional liturgical color is purple, the purple of majesty which heralds the coming of the King of Kings.

Advent Wreath

As a symbolic object, the Advent wreath with four candles serves well to designate this season. The wreath is constructed of evergreens, an ancient symbol of immortality, life and growth. The circle of the wreath is unending and symbolic of eternity—God was  and is and always will be. The four candles represent the four Sundays of Advent. Purple is the appropriate color of these candles, following the liturgical color of the season. On the first Sunday of Advent one candle is lit; two are lit for the second Sunday, and so on until the fourth week. Sometimes a fifth candle is added in the center on Christmas Eve, which is the last day of Advent. This candle is white, the color of purity and joy, and is known as the "Christ Candle".

The candles, when lighted, symbolize the Coming of Christ, the Light of the World. (See CANDLE in the Christmas section.)

The Advent wreath usually rests on a horizontal surface. This is especially appropriate when it is used in the home as the center for daily Advent devotions. The wreath is the successor to the ancient corona or crown chandelier, which hung from the ceiling of the chancel. So it is sometimes hung horizontally by four chains which converge at the ceiling, each pair making a triangle, one of the oldest symbols of the Holy Trinity. (See TRIANGLE in the section on Feasts of the Pentecost Season.)

Alpha and Omega

An ancient symbol appropriate to the two themes of Advent may be found in  the two Greek letters Alpha and Omega, "the first and the last, the beginning and the end" of the Greek alphabet. Advent prepares us for the beginning and the end of the Christian epoch. In the last chapter of the Bible (Revelation 22:12-13) Christ speaks these words from heaven: "Behold, I am coming soon, bringing my recompense, to repay every one for what he has done. I am the Alpha and the Omega, the first and the last, the beginning and the end." This verse makes the word a title of Christ and a fitting symbol to represent his first and second comings.

Christ is the Word. "He was in the beginning with God; all things were made through him, and without him was not anything made that was made" (John 1:2-3). At the conclusion of his gospel, Matthew gives these words of Christ: "Lo, I am with you always, to the close of the age" (Matthew 28:20).

This symbol is often accompanied by other symbols for Christ to give an added meaning. Used in this connection are the cross, the *chi rho* (from the first two letters of the Greek *christos,* "the Christ"), or a combination of the two.

Darkness

Light is a symbol of God's presence and darkness, its opposite, a symbol of his absence. Darkness stands for a lack of salvation which is overcome by the arrival of Christ the Messiah.

"The people who walked in
    darkness have seen a great light;
those who dwelt in a land of deep
    darkness, on them has light
    shined." (Isa. 9:2)

"The night is far gone, the day is at hand. Let us then cast off the works of darkness, and put on the armor of light" (Romans 13:12). See LIGHT in the Christmas section.

Elijah

According to a common view of the Jews in the first century A.D., a forerunner of the messiah would appear to announce his coming. Basing their idea on the book of Malachi, many thought that this forerunner would be Elijah returned to earth. The verses related to this expectation are:

"Behold, I will send my messenger to prepare the way before me, and the Lord whom you seek will suddenly come to his temple." (Malachi 3:1)

"Behold, I will send you Elijah the prophet before the great and terrible day of the Lord comes." (Malachi 4:5)

Jesus seems to have considered John

the Baptist as fulfilling the role of Elijah, as for example this remark about John: "And if you are willing to accept it, he is Elijah who is to come." (Matthew 11:14) Or the reply to his disciples' question, "'Why do the scribes say that first Elijah must come?' and he said to them, 'Elijah does come first to restore all things . . . But I tell you that Elijah has come . . .'" (Mark 9:11-13)

A flaming chariot, or more simply a flaming wheel, may be used as a symbol for Elijah (II Kings 2:1-12).

Jesse Tree

See TITLES OF JESUS CHRIST; also JESSE TREE in Christmas section.

John The Baptist

Because John the Baptist began his preaching before Jesus did and indicated Jesus as "he who is coming after me" and the one who "is mightier than I" (Matthew 3:11), he is called the forerunner. He made the announcement of Jesus' advent or coming. He is the central figure in the gospels of the second and third Sundays of Advent.

In art John the Baptist sometimes carries a lamb in his arms and holds a scroll bearing the Latin words: *Ecce Agnus Dei* ("Behold the Lamb of God" John 1:36). He traditionally holds a cross made of reeds, often with a banner attached to it. Because the Virgin Mary and Elizabeth were related (see Luke 1:36), their sons,

Jesus and John, are often shown as children in the same scene. See LAMB in Holy Week section and BANNER in Christmas section.

Last Judgment

The message of Advent is that Christ has come, still comes, and will come again to judge the living and the dead. Paintings and sculptures of the Last Judgment usually show Christ in majesty on his heavenly throne. In earlier scenes (until the twelfth century) he is surrounded by the four winged creatures of Revelation 4:6-7, man, lion, ox, eagle (starting at Christ's right shoulder and going counterclockwise in the order of Ezekiel 1:10).

In modern times these four creatures usually symbolize the four Gospels or Evangelists (Matthew, Mark, Luke, John). In the Middle Ages they also represented Christ's Nativity or Incarnation (man), his sacrificial Death (ox), his Resurrection (lion) and his Ascension (eagle). See EAGLE and LION in Easter-Ascension section.

In some later art the Virgin Mary appears kneeling at Christ's right hand and St. John kneels at the left. They are interceding for men. St. Michael, the angel of death, with his scales, sometimes appears prominently. According to the parable of the great judgment (sheep and goats) in Matthew 25:31-46, when the souls are shown gathered in judgment the elect appear on Christ's right, the place of honor, and the damned on his left.

Tau Cross

The letter T in Greek *(tau)* gives its name to the two-armed cross which is sometimes called the Old Testament or prophetic cross and so also the Advent Cross. It is regarded as the form of the staff which Moses used in the wilderness for displaying  the serpent of bronze. "So Moses made a bronze serpent, and set it on a pole; and if a serpent bit a man, he would look at the bronze serpent and live." (Numbers 21:9) Jesus referred to this in John 3:14, "as Moses lifted up the serpent in the wilderness, so must the Son of Man be lifted up." See CROSS in Holy Week and Feasts of the Pentecost Season sections.

Titles of Jesus Christ

The Advent hymn, "O Come, O Come, Emmanuel," bestows on Jesus the Messiah a series of titles taken from Holy Scripture and from the Advent antiphons sung at vespers from December 17th until Christmas Eve.

 (1) *O Sapientia*, "O Wisdom." The concept of wisdom personified as found in Proverbs 8:22-31, and this made possible the application of Christ, the wisdom from on high through whom all things were made. A burning lamp is a traditional symbol for wisdom.

(2) *O Adonai*, "O Lord of Might," A Hebrew title of God. A substitute for his name, which could not be spoken. The burning bush is often used as a symbol in  connection with this title. The antiphon itself gives us this thought: "O Adonai and Leader of the house of Israel, who appeared to Moses in the fire of the flaming bush and gavest him the law on Sinai; come and redeem us by thy outstretched arm."

(3) *O Radix Jesse*, "Rod" or "Root of Jesse." The angel told the Virgin Mary that Jesus would inherit "the throne of his father David"  (Luke 1:32). Jesse was David's father. Jesus is thus honored as a king. In Revelation 22:16 Jesus says, "I am the root and the offspring of David." A symbolic representation is a plant with flower (Jesus) and root (Jesse). A six-pointed star may represent Jesse and David, a *chi rho* or *iota chi* Christ. See JESSE TREE in Christmas section.

(4) *O Clavis David*, "Key of David." A key is a symbol of authority. The phrase comes from Revelation 3:7, where it  is taken from the Old Testament messianic passage in Isaiah 22:22.

(5) *O Oriens*, "Dayspring from on high" (Luke 1:78 KJV). This refers to the dawning of the mes-  sianic age, and recalls Malachi 4:2, "The sun of righteousness shall rise with healing in its wings."

(6) *O Rex Gentium*, "King of Nations." Christ is referred to as "King of kings and Lord of lords" in I Timothy 6:15 and Revela- tion 19:16. See CROWN in Trinity Sunday Section.

(7) *O Emmanuel*, "God with us." Matthew 1:23 refers to Isaiah 7:14, "A young woman shall conceive and bear a son, and shall call his name Emmanuel." For ap-  propriate symbols, see CANDLE and CRIB in the Christmas section.

For other descriptive titles of Christ, see MESSIAH, PRINCE OF PEACE, SUN OF RIGHTEOUSNESS and SAVIOR in the Christmas section. See also REDEEMER and LAMB OF GOD in the Holy Week section.

Christmas and Epiphany

The Twelve Days of Christmas begin with the feast of Christmas on December 25 and end with the feast of the Epiphany on January 6. (The Twelve Nights begin on Christmas Eve and end on Epiphany Eve.) According to the Church calendar, Christmastide is concluded on January 5 and "The Epiphany" on January 6 begins an Epiphany season which varies in length according to the date of Easter.

On Christmas Day the world remembers the Incarnation of our Lord, that is, the assuming of human form by God in Jesus Christ. The Book of Common Prayer puts it this way: Christ "by the mighty power of the Holy Spirit was made perfect Man of the flesh of the Virgin Mary his mother;" and calls it "the mystery of the Word made flesh" (John 1:1ff).

The Christmas season, which begins with the Nativity on December 25, includes some special days. These honor St. Stephen, the first Christian martyr (December 26), St. John, apostle and evangelist (December 27), and the Holy Innocents killed at Bethlehem (December 28). (Note that the revised Church calendar gives precedence to the First Sunday after Christmas, possibly resulting in the postponement by one day of one or more of the three.) To provide symbols for these saints' days, the following are suggested:

St. Stephen, who was stoned to death - stones and a palm branch;

St. John as apostle - a "poisoned" chalice with a serpent within; as evangelist - an eagle;

Holy Innocents - starry crowns of martyrdom and lilies of purity.

Epiphany season focuses the Christian's attention on the manifestations or appearances of Christ as a divine being. The three traditional manifestations, since the early centuries of the Church, have been:

The Nativity of Christ and the Adoration of the Wise Men;

The Baptism of Christ when the Spirit descended on him;

The first miracle at Cana when at a marriage Jesus turned water into wine.

References to these manifestations are made in the first two stanzas of the hymn, "Songs of thankfulness and praise," by Christopher Wordsworth.

According to the three-year lectionary now employed in several church bodies the Epiphany season is also a period for remembering that

Jesus called disciples to help him and asked them to be "fishers of men;"

Jesus healed the sick in body and in mind;

Jesus was transfigured on the mountain (as recalled every year in the Gospel for the Last Sunday after Epiphany).

Scholars now are inclined to believe that Epiphany originated in the East as a festival commemorating both the Birth and the Baptism of Jesus Christ, while in the West a little later Christmas (without Epiphany) was chosen to remember the Nativity and the Adoration of the Magi. Eventually both festivals came into all church calendars. In the West some churches were honoring the Magi on Epiphany instead of Christmas and this custom finally became the rule in all the Roman churches. Liturgically everything connected with the Lucan account of the Adoration of the Shepherds belongs with Christmas and everything connected with the Matthean account of the Star in the East and the Wise Men belongs with Epiphany. But popular favor has reverted to the earlier idea of including the Magi in the observance of December 25. For the listing of symbols it seems suitable to take both seasons and festivals together.

The Annunciation to the Virgin Mary might be taken as an Advent theme, but since the scene is included in many of the older Nativity pictures and triptychs and in Christmas pageants, its symbolism is discussed in this section.

The earliest representations of the Nativity and the Visit of the Magi up to about 400 A.D. were highly symbolic. The Christ Child was a divine king to be adored by the shepherds representing the Jews, the Magi representing the Gentiles and the ox and ass representing the natural world. The scene is shown in the open. Beginning in the fifth century Western Nativities included a manger in an open shed while in the East the Child was put in a cave.

Much fuller symbolism came in with the Renaissance artists as they depicted the Bible story. They introduced elaborate architectural forms and the animal and plant life which employ more subtle symbolism. In modern times there has been a trend back to simplicity.

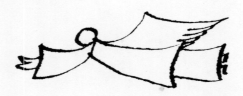

Angel

Angels kneeling near the Holy Family indicate adoration due a divinity. The herald angel sometimes seen floating in space with right hand raised represents the announcement to the shepherds and is a true Nativity angel. An angel in a circle in the sky stands for the star seen by the Magi. (See GABRIEL and STAR)

Annunciation

The name given to the event and scene of the announcement by the angel Gabriel to the Virgin Mary of the Incarnation of Jesus Christ (Luke 1:26-32). The scene may appear as a part of a larger Nativity picture or as one of the three scenes on a triptych. According to one tradition the Virgin Mary is an enclosed garden (Song of Songs 4:12) and therefore flowers, such as lilies, must be in the scene. See GABRIEL and LILY.

Apple

By tradition the apple is the fruit of the Paradise Tree. It is used sometimes as a symbol of Christ, the new (or second) Adam. In some medieval Christmas plays there appeared a  Paradise Tree adorned with apples. This may be an early version of the Christmas Tree. See CHRISTMAS TREE.

Ass

The ass and the ox, although not mentioned in the Gospels, usually appear in Nativity scenes and represent the animal creation paying homage to the Christ Child. It is sometimes claimed that the ass stands for the Gentile world and the ox for the Jewish. The earliest account of the two animals adoring the Child occurs in the apocryphal Gospel of Pseudo-Matthew (chap. xiv) and some Roman Christian sarcophagi depict them. The suggestion for placing them there may have come from Isaiah 1:3—"The ox knows its owner, and the ass its master's crib." (See OX)

Augustus Caesar (Roman emperor 27 B.C.—14 A.D.)

There is a legend depicted by some artists that the Emperor Augustus inquired of the Tiburtine Sibyl (a prophetess) if there was anyone living as great as he. In reply she showed him her vision of the sun at noon and in its center a maiden holding a child in her arms. She said: "This child is a greater lord than you are; worship him." The story is recorded in the *Golden Legend*. This scene represents the manifestation of Christ to the West as the Journey of the Magi does for the East.

Aureole

This artistic device is a halo of radiance encircling the body or head of one of the three Persons of the Trinity: the Father, the Son, or the Holy Spirit. It is a symbol of divinity and supreme power. As the origin of the word implies (Latin *aurum,* gold) the aureole is usually shown in gold representing rays of light. Like the nimbus or glory, the idea is of pagan origin. Romans used it for their gods and for deified emperors. (See NIMBUS)

Balthasar or Balthazzar

One of the three Wise Men. See MAGI.

Banner

Banners with symbols on them which are seen in religious pictures sometimes identify persons depicted. John the Baptist may hold a staff with a banner on which there is a cross of reed—his symbol. Banners in the form of streamers or ribbons are used as a background for quotations having to do with the subject of the picture.

Baptism of Jesus Christ

Although the Gospels do not say that the Holy Spirit descended upon Christ while he was in the water, the scene is frequently pictured that way. The Gospels do tell us that when Jesus had been baptized he went up out of the water, the heavens opened, and then he saw the Spirit of God descending like a dove (Matthew 3:16, Mark 1:10, Luke 3:22). Early Eastern Christians often added the hand of God with rays of light issuing from it. They also liked to put in a figure of the god of the Jordan fleeing from the river, and two or more ministering angels. The idea of the personified Jordan fleeing was justified by reference to Psalm 114:3,

"The sea looked and fled,
Jordan turned back."

(Actually this is a reference to Joshua and his followers crossing the river in Joshua 3.) Occasionally a dragon is shown in the water. This idea comes from Psalm 74:13, "thou didst break the heads of the dragons on the waters."

Bethlehem

The name means "house of bread." As David's childhood home it was often called the City of David (I Samuel 17:12). In Micah 5:2 (quoted in Matthew 2:6) the prediction is made that Bethlehem will be the birthplace of a shepherd king. Bethlehem is in the province of Judea.

"And you, O Bethlehem, in the land of Judah,
are by no means least among the rulers of Judah,
for from you shall come a ruler
who will govern my people Israel."

Caesar Augustus (see AUGUSTUS)

Camel

Since the camel provided a means of travel and beast of burden in the Orient, its appearance signifies a person from the East and usually one of royal mien. Therefore it is appropriate in scenes of the Wise Men. *The Golden Legend* says that the Magi used dromedaries because they travel swiftly.

Camels are highly valued in desert areas and places that are dry at certain seasons of the year. A man's wealth was measured sometimes by the camels he owned. They would be especially useful to men traveling great distances.

The Renaissance paintings of the Visit of the Magi seem to have been influenced by the following two Bible verses.

She [the queen of Sheba] came to Jerusalem with a very great retinue, with camels bearing spices, and very much gold, and precious stones. (I Kings 10:2)

A multitude of camels shall cover you,
    the young camels of Midian and Ephah;
    all those from Sheba shall come.
They shall bring gold and frankincense,
    and shall proclaim the praise of the Lord. (Isaiah 60:6)

Candle

When lit the candle reminds us that Jesus said: "I am the light of the world" (John 8:12), and that Simeon called him "a light to lighten the Gentiles" (Luke 2:32 KJV). Yule candles, made extra large to keep burning throughout the night of Christmas Eve, are symbols of good luck as long as they remain burning.

Caskets

When the wisemen were "opening their treasures" (Matthew 2:11), they were taking the gifts of gold, frankincense and myrrh out of their traveling containers. These caskets are sometimes shown in Epiphany pictures. See MAGI.

Caspar

Another name for Jaspar. See MAGI.

Cave

While not biblical, the cave traditionally indicates the shelter in which Christ was born. A cave near the ancient marketplace of Bethlehem was being pointed out as the birthplace during the second century. Justin Martyr mentions it (about 150 A.D.). A century later Origen knew of it. The church historian Eusebius tells that the Empress Helena made of the cave a splendid sanctuary. Her son Constantine built a basilica over it. By 400 A.D. St. Jerome had settled in a monastery nearby and was sometimes disturbed in his studies by the crowds of pilgrims visiting this cave.

Apocryphal gospels mention the cave as the site of Christ's birth and one (Gospel of Pseudo-Matthew) states that on the third day Mary and the Child moved from the cave into the stable where the baby was placed in the manger.

The cave often appears in Nativity pictures. It helps to emphasize the humble estate of Mary and Joseph and the humility of the Son of God's taking flesh (the Incarnation). See STABLE.

Christ

This word comes from the Greek word *Christos,* meaning "the anointed." It is a translation of *Mashiah* (messiah). The early Church applied the title Christ to Jesus of Nazareth and it thus became part of his name. Originally the kings of Israel (Saul, David, Solomon) were anointed on the head when assuming the kingship. The rite was intended to transfer to the man anointed some of the holiness, virtue and spirit of God. The New Testament indicates that the early Christians considered Jesus as the Messiah or Christ looked for by the Jewish nation.

Christmas Day

Christmas is Christ-mass, a religious festival honoring the Nativity of Our Lord Jesus Christ. The day and month of his birth are unrecorded. The Church fixed on December 25 in Rome in the middle of the fourth century apparently as a counter-attraction for Christians to the birthday of the *Sol Invictus* (Unconquered Sun) of Mithraism then being celebrated at Rome. December 25 was the winter solstice according to the Julian calendar. Christ has been called the "Sun of Righteousness" who shall rise "with healing in his wings" (Malachi 4:2 KJV). This beautiful image comes from a symbol in Egypt and the Near East in which the sun disk with wings represents protection and blessing.

Christmas Rose

Helleborus niger is the botanical name of this winter blooming flower. Being white, it symbolizes the purity of the Virgin Mary and the Christ Child.

Christmas Tree

The tree as a religious symbol takes us back to the very beginning of history. The Tree of Life enjoyed great popularity as a symbol for many centuries. There was one in the Garden of Eden along with the Tree of Knowledge which caused the fall of Adam and Eve. In the Middle Ages the Cross was regarded as the Tree of Life.

A legend in the Gospel of Pseudo-Matthew tells that when the Holy Family was on the way to Egypt they were passing a palm tree laden with fruit. Mary wished for some, but the fruit was up at the top, out of reach. The infant Jesus commanded the tree to bow down and it did so, enabling them to gather the fruit.

In medieval religious Christmas plays the Tree of Paradise was sometimes shown. One on record happens to be a juniper adorned with apples and ribbons. Sometimes Christ was regarded as the Tree of Paradise. Christ as the Light of the World and the Tree of Life may have given a Christian meaning to the honoring of the tree in paganism. At any rate, the Paradise Tree impresses some authorities as one source of the Christmas Tree.

Other possible sources of the Christmas Tree can be found in the

Roman custom of decorating houses with evergreens on the Kalends of January (New Year's Day) and a popular belief that on Christmas Eve apple and other fruit trees produced blossoms. This latter may be related to the custom of cutting cherry and other flowering boughs to put in water in the warm indoors for Christmas blooming.

Certainly a decorated and lighted tree helps impress on our emotions the joy connected with the Coming of Christ. See GLASTONBURY THORN, JESSE TREE and TREE ORNAMENTS.

Crib or Crèche

The original crib in which the Christ Child was laid was a manger in the stable, a sign of the humble surroundings of his birth. In imitation of this the Church of St. Maria Maggiore at Rome had a wooden replica at which the midnight Christmas mass was celebrated. This crib is known as the *praesepe* (manger). The popular Christmas crèche at churches and in homes creates a tableau of Jesus in the stable crib at Bethlehem, depicting scenes described by Luke and Matthew.

David

As the "anointed" (and in this sense a messianic) king of Israel David founded a royal house destined to continue as the rulers of the nation. The idea that the future Messiah would be a descendant of David, of the "house of David," received strength from Isaiah (chap. 7) and Micah (5:2-4). This accounts for the New Testament interest in citing David as the great ancestor of the Christ, beginning with his birth in Bethlehem, "the city of David" (See Luke 1:69, 2:4,11). Emblems for David include the harp or lyre on which he played (I Samuel 16:16 and I Chronicles 13:8), and the head of the lion which he slew (I Samuel 17:34f).

Dove

At the Baptism of Jesus the presence of the Holy Spirit became evident by the appearance of a dove descending upon him (Matthew 3:16, Mark 1:10, Luke 3:22). This is the usual symbol for the Spirit of God. See DOVE in the section on Feasts of the Pentecost Season.

Epiphany

The name comes from the Greek word *epiphaneia*, "appearance." In Western churches this feast commemorates the revelation or manifestation of Christ to the Gentiles as portrayed by the Wise Men from the East. In the East Epiphany served as the original festival of the Incarnation. In some ancient churches Epiphany also commemorated the Baptism of our Lord and the birth of light ("The true light that enlightens every man was coming into the world." John 1:9).

Frankincense

Gums and spices which may be burned to produce a fragrant smoke as a feature of religious ceremonies are called incense. Frankincense is a particular kind of incense of high quality. It comes from trees of the genus *Boswellia* found in Africa and Asia. It was highly esteemed by the Greeks, Romans, and Jews. Since it was an accompaniment of worship, it symbolizes divinity.

See MAGI.

Gabriel

He is one of the archangels and is frequently dignified with the title of Saint. Gabriel is the angel of the Annunciation to the Virgin Mary, while by tradition Raphael is the angel who brought the news of Jesus' birth to the shepherds. Luke specifies Gabriel as the angel "sent from God" to tell Mary that she would bear a son to be called Jesus (Luke 1:26). Earlier the same angel appeared to Zechariah, father of John the Baptist, saying, "I am Gabriel, who stand in the presence of God; and I was sent to you to bring you this good news" (Luke 1:19).

Early representations of the Annunciation show Gabriel wearing a crown and carrying a scepter to indicate sovereignty. Later he is subordinated to the Virgin and holds in place of the scepter a lily which signifies the purity of Mary. See ANNUNCIATION.

Garland

Christmas garlands and evergreens apparently came in as a carry-over from the customs of Greece and Rome. Decorating with evergreens formed a part of the Kalends (or New Year's)celebrations observed by Christians for several centuries in the Christian era. The garlands were often made of some evergreen ma-terial and were decorated with fruit; or they were strings of fruit similar to the cranberry strings used on Christmas trees today. Evergreens remind us of the preservation of life through the deadness of winter.

Gaspard

Another name for Jaspar. See MAGI.

Gate

The Jews had a number of psalms for festival use. One that was probably intended for the New Year is Psalms 24. Verse 7 reads:

"Lift up your heads, O gates!
and be lifted up, O ancient doors!
that the King of glory may come in."
Christians have expanded this reference to include the Messiah. A hymn based on this psalm, written by Georg Weissel for the First Sunday of Advent, begins:

Lift up your heads, ye mighty gates;
Behold the King of Glory waits!
The King of Kings is drawing near;
The Saviour of the world is here.

Gifts

The first Christmas gifts were those presented to the Christ Child by the Wise Men. See MAGI.

Saint Nicholas, the original Santa Claus, secretly left gifts of gold at a poor man's house so that he could honorably marry off his daughters with dowries. This legend was cited as an example of the good saint's love of any of God's children in distress. Later Saint Nicholas became the patron saint of school children and, according to tradition in some countries, Saint Nicholas or Santa Claus leaves gifts secretly during the night.

Possibly the Roman Kalends of January custom of gift giving is partly responsible for Christmas gifts. E. K. Chambers shows the symbolism of some of the Kalends gifts: "honeyed things, that the year of the recipient might be full of sweetness, lamps that it might be full of light, copper, silver and gold that wealth might flow in amain" (*Medieval Stage*, I. 238).

Glastonbury Thorn

This hawthorn bush blooms annually at the Christmas season. According to legend Joseph of Arimathea, the man responsible for burying the body of Jesus, migrated to England and settled at Glastonbury. He stuck his staff into the ground there, and it grew into a tree, and blossomed at Christmas. This goes along with the general idea that blossoming boughs and trees accompanied Christ's birth. See CHRISTMAS TREE.

Glory of the Lord

This glory (Luke 2:9) which the shepherds saw is the brightness or splendor of God revealing his presence. The prophet Ezekiel had a vision of God on his throne. In concluding his description of this he says, "Such was the appearance of the likeness of the glory of the Lord." (Ezekiel 1:28) At Jesus' Transfiguration Peter, James and John looking at him "saw his glory." (Luke 9:32)

The Hebrew "shekinah", which the Jews believed would appear with the Messiah, is roughly equivalent to the New Testament "glory." Hebrews held a belief in God's personal presence on earth and their use of the term "shekinah" or glory carried with it the idea of God's presence among men.

At his conversion St. Paul saw "a light from heaven, brighter than the sun." (Acts 26:13) This helped convince him that Jesus, the Lord, was actually there speaking to him.

Gold

Gold represents wealth and royalty. As a gift to the Christ Child it symbolizes his kingship. See MAGI.

Hand or Hands

When shown at the top of the scene of Jesus' Baptism the hand or hands with fingers extended downwards indicates the presence of God the Father and his blessing on the event. This is the artist's rendering of the words "Thou art my beloved son; with thee I am well pleased" (Mark 1:11; also Matthew 3:17; Luke 3:22). See BAPTISM OF JESUS CHRIST.

Herod

The aged King of Judea at the time of Jesus' birth and the visit of the Magi. He died at about the age of seventy in 4 B.C. Because of his mad desire to kill the Christ Child and the slaughter of the innocent male babies in Bethlehem, he is popularly the embodiment of evil.

Holly

Holly (*Ilex*) has thorny leaves which remain green when branches are cut, and the fruit is a red berry. Because of this it is symbolic of the crown of thorns and drops of blood on the Savior's head. By tradition it is also the burning bush which became sacred to Moses. Although holly reminds us of the Passion, it is also one of the evergreens which from ancient times has been deemed appropriate for celebrating the great winter festival.

I H S, I H C

These three letters stand for the name "Jesus" in Greek. There is no J in the Greek and Latin alphabets; so I is used instead. H is the capital E in Greek, and C is the cursive script for S. So these are the first two and the last letters (or the first three) of JESUS. Scribes used a line or bar over the middle letter, IHS, to indicate an abbreviation. This bar shown later became a Latin cross over the H. (Periods should never be used after any of these letters.)

This symbol becomes appropriate to the Christmas season because it was eight days after his birth that our Lord received his name—a date which is remembered on January 1 in our calendar. Various names for this festival within the Twelve Days of Christmas are: "The Holy Name of Our Lord Jesus Christ," "The Circumcision of Christ," and "The Octave Day of Christmas."

The Scripture verse which applies is Luke 2:21—"And at the end of eight days, when he was circumcised, he was called Jesus."

Incarnation

When God the Son took human form and became Jesus Christ on earth, it was  God becoming incarnate (made flesh). The term expresses the belief that in Jesus God "Has visited and redeemed his people" (Luke 1:68). The Incarnation became evident to the Virgin Mary at the Annunciation and to the world at the Nativity and the Epiphany. Renaissance artists used the swallow as a symbol of the Incarnation in scenes of the Annunciation and the Nativity. These birds nest under eaves and in holes of walls. See SWALLOW in Easter section.

Inn

Luke says, "There was no place for them in the inn." Jesus was born in more humble quarters, which tradition regards as either a stable or a cave. Artists sometimes show the Holy Family in or near a cave or shed. A house near them is not always meant to be the Bethlehem inn. It may represent the home of Jesse, father of David, now being superseded.

Jaspar (or CASPAR or GASPARD)

One of the three Magi. See MAGI.

24

Jesse and Jesse Tree

The father of David, named Jesse, lived in Bethlehem and his old hut, in ruins, often appears in Nativity scenes. The lineage of Jesus Christ is traced back through David to Jesse (Matthew 1:6ff.; Luke 2:4ff.) and the prophecy in Isaiah 11:1 is sometimes cited in this connection:

"There shall come forth a shoot from the stump of Jesse, and a branch shall grow out of his roots."

A symbol of this lineage is found in the Jesse tree. In this Jesse is represented in a recumbent position with a tree or vine growing out of his loins. Attached to the tree are symbols of various personages in the line of descent. The Virgin Mary and the child Jesus usually appear at the top.

Luke tells that Jesus happened to be born in Bethlehem because Joseph was of the house of David and went back to Bethlehem to be enrolled.

Notice the reference to Jesse in the Christmas hymn, "I know a rose-tree springing."

The symbolism of the Tree of Jesse was suggested by the Latin text of the above verse from Isaiah 11:1, plus verse 10. The Douai translation of this runs:

And there shall come forth a rod out of the root of Jesse, and a flower shall rise up out of his root. . . . And the spirit of the Lord shall be the root of Jesse, whom standeth for an ensign of the people.

Medieval interpretations made the rod (Latin *virga*) mean the Virgin, the root mean tree and the flower Christ. As Ambrose said: "The root is the family of the Jews, the stem Mary, the flower of Mary is Christ."

See TITLES OF JESUS CHRIST in Advent section.

Kalends (Calends) of January

Kalends refers to the first day of a Roman month. In January this was the Roman New Year's Day and a time for celebrating. This festival covered a period of three days. Some of its customs, such as decorating with greenery and giving gifts, have been appropriated for Christmas.

Kings (see MAGI)

Laurel

As a Christmas decoration laurel came into favor very early because of its use by Greeks and Romans and especially at the Kalends of January (New Year's). From laurel, wreaths used to be made to crown the victors in sporting events. Thus it symbolizes triumph and victory. The fact that laurel is an evergreen and does not wilt gives it also an association with eternity and everlasting life. According to old customs laurel makes an appropriate material for Christmas wreaths and garlands.

Leopard

Sometimes in depictions of the Adoration of the Magi a leopard is shown. As a symbol of sin or the devil, in this case it is meant to remind us that the Incarnation of Christ was necessary for the redemption from sin. See DEVIL in the Lent section.

Light

Christ called himself "the Light of the World" (John 8:12). He added, "he who follows me will not walk in darkness, but will have the light of life." Darkness stands for evil and sin. Light represents righteousness and the presence of God. Light is symbolic of Christ. In the calendar year Christ appeared at the darkest time when days are just beginning to get longer and brighter.

In Nativity scenes light often fills the cave or stable and according to the Protevangelium of James the bright light came from the babe in the manger. Christmas candles and lights originally stood for the coming of Christ into the world. They are also symbolic of joy and righteousness.

See DARKNESS in the Advent section.

Lily

As a symbol of purity this flower belongs particularly to the Virgin Mary. It is often shown in pictures of the Annunciation either in a vase between the Virgin and the angel or in Gabriel's hand. Thus the lily in an angel's hand designates the Archangel Gabriel. See ANNUNCIATION and GABRIEL.

Magi

Their Profession. The Wise Men of Matthew 2 are not kings but priestly students of the stars, men accustomed to interpreting the significance for human affairs of the movements of heavenly bodies and the meaning of dreams. They were not Jews, but represent pagan religions, or as the Jews called such people, Gentiles.

The idea that they were also kings came out of Eastern Christianity as a result of several Old Testament verses thought to be predictions. The chief of these is Psalms 72:10,

> May the kings of Tarshish and of the isles render him tribute,
> May the kings of Sheba and Seba bring gifts.

The kings represent distant nations come to pay homage. Other passages suggesting them as kings include Isaiah 60:3,

> Nations shall come to your light,
> And kings to the brightness of your rising.

Their Number and Names. Oriental tradition places their number at twelve and assigns names unknown in the West. In early Christian art they are depicted in symmetry, in even numbers, two, four or  six. By Abelard's time in the Middle Ages the idea of the three gifts had fixed their number at three. By the same time their Latin names had been decided upon as Jaspar, Melchior and Balthasar.

Their Nationality and Race. Matthew tells only that they came from the East. Early representations picture them in Persian dress. The countries mentioned in Psalm 72:10 (Tarshish, Sheba, Seba) and Isaiah 60:6 (Sheba) provided material for the medieval legend that they were:

*King of Tarshish, land of merchants in the West, who brought gold.

*King of Arabia and Nubia, who brought frankincense.

* King of Seba, land of spices and precious gums in the East, who brought myrrh.

Some medieval sermons state that the three Magi, who were prefigured by the three sons of Noah (Shem, Ham and Japheth), represent the three races of mankind (from Europe, Asia and Africa) rendering homage to Christ.

Their Ages and Appearance. Originally the facial appearance of the Magi depended on the area of the artistic creation. In the West they were shown as beardless, but in the East the three were either all bearded or depicted individually as heavily bearded, small-bearded and beardless. Along with this latter tradition went the idea that the three represented old age, middle age and youth. In a legend recorded in Bede's works Balthasar has dark skin and a full beard, Jaspar is young and beardless with a ruddy countenance, and Melchior is middle-aged, sallow and small-bearded.

Their Gifts. The early Church Fathers, writing in the first half of the third century, cited significant reasons for the choice of gold, frankincense and myrrh; that is, gold signifies royalty, incense divinity and myrrh mortal humanity. Irenaeus said that they brought "myrrh because it was he who should die and be buried for the mortal human race; gold because he was a king, 'of whose kingdom is no end;' and frankincense because he was God."

Tradition varies as to which name goes with which gift. According to the legend found in Bede's writings, Jaspar presented incense, Balthasar offered myrrh and Melchior brought gold.

See FRANKINCENSE, GOLD and MYRRH.

Manger

See CRIB.

Melchior

One of the Wise Men. See MAGI.

Messiah

This is the Hebrew term for Christ. The Old Testament taught the Jews to expect salvation or deliverance to come from God at the hands of a kingly messiah. The one to bring salvation is also called the Savior. Joseph was told that Jesus "will save his people from their sins" (Matthew 1:21), and the angel announced to the shepherds the birth of "a Savior, who is Christ the Lord" (Luke 2:11).

Mistletoe

Once connected with the death of Baldur in Scandinavian lore, mistletoe in the Christian world became a symbol of joy and good will. Some have thought that the religious ceremony of the kiss of peace may have contributed to the custom of using this bough for a kissing privilege.

Myrrh

This gum resin comes from Africa and Arabia. Its taste is bitter and pungent. Ancient peoples valued it as an ingredient for perfumes and unguents. It symbolizes a suffering body or death because it is used to anoint bodies before burial. See MAGI.

Nimbus

Taken from the Latin word for "cloud," the nimbus surrounding the head or body signifies a holy person. It is also known as the "glory." The usual color is gold, but other colors such as red, blue, or green are sometimes found. It represents divine glory. See AUREOLE and GLORY OF THE LORD.

Noel or Nowel

Noel is a French word probably derived from the Latin *natalis (dies)*, day of nativity, referring to the Nativity of Christ. The word has become an expression of joy in English carols.

Ox

Along with the ass this animal appears in many Nativity scenes. In early representations they are on their knees in an attitude of worship. This idea finds literary expression in the Gospel of Pseudo-Matthew which says:

". . . and an ox and an ass worshipped him. Then was fulfilled that which was said by the prophet, Isaiah, 'The ox knows his owner and the ass his master's crib.' (Is. 1:3) Thus the beasts, ox and ass, with him between them, unceasingly worshipped him. Then was fulfilled that which was said by the prophet Habakkuk, 'Between two beasts are you known.'" (Habakkuk 3:2, Septuagint trans.)

Pack or Sack

A legend of St. Nicholas tells of his using a bag of gold as a gift for poverty-stricken maidens. Santa Claus, who is a modern equivalent of the good saint, must have a container to hold his gifts. Like his predecessor he uses a cloth bag, grown into a large pack or sack. See GIFT and ST. NICHOLAS.

Paradise Tree

See CHRISTMAS TREE.

Peacock

A symbol of immortality and eternal life. It sometimes appears in Nativity scenes. According to ancient legend the peacock's flesh does not decay when dead. Roman coins depicted emperors being carried to heaven by eagles and empresses by peacocks. See also PEACOCK in Easter section.

Pomegranate

This fruit, sometimes seen in the hand of the Christ Child (as in the Adoration of the Magi by Fra Angelico), gets its meaning of the hope of resurrection from the classical myth of Persephone. As wife of Pluto and goddess of the underworld, Persephone could not live in the upper world as her mother Demeter desired, but could only return periodically for the portion of the year when vegetation exists above ground. Her only food in the underworld had been seeds from a pomegranate which she shared with her husband Pluto, but because she had eaten this in the underworld she was required to spend part of each year there.

Prince of Peace

This is one of the titles of the Messiah found in Isaiah 9:6. The whole verse reads:
For unto us a child is born,
to us a son is given;
and the government will be upon his
shoulder,
and his name will be called
"Wonderful Counselor, Mighty God,
Everlasting Father, Prince of Peace."
Jesus came to bring "peace on earth, goodwill to men." The Prince of Peace, it was hoped, would do more than obliterate the desire and need for war. He would also bring harmony and positive well-being to his people.

See TITLES OF JESUS CHRIST in the Advent section.

Reindeer

These animals, according to the old tradition, draw the sleigh of Santa Claus. They seem to have come to America for the Christmas festivities in the pleasant imagination of Clement Moore who wrote the popular poem, "A Visit from St. Nicholas." Reindeer were domesticated in Scandinavia many years ago and they were trained to wear harness and draw sleighs. According to Moore St. Nicholas "was dressed all in fur, from his head to his foot." The conclusion can easily be drawn that the animals and the man represent winter and the far northern regions. See SAINT NICHOLAS.

Ruins

In Renaissance paintings of the Nativity and of the Visit of the Magi ruined or incomplete buildings, walls, or gateways may be shown. This happens partly from the growing interest at that time in classical architecture and the remains of old Roman buildings. But a tradition prevailed that a house in ruins at the time of Jesus' birth was once inhabited by Jesse, the father of David, and was near the spot where David tended the sheep. Since Jesse's time the house had become a shed only partially protected from the weather. Jesse's house falling to ruins typified the old dispensation which with Christ's birth was being superseded.

Saint Nicholas and Santa Claus

Santa Claus is an American name, derived from the Dutch, for the original

Saint Nicholas. He was a fourth century Bishop of Myra in Asia Minor. On his day, December 6, Dutch children look for the kindly saint dressed in bishop's robes as he rides around on a white horse while he distributes gifts. Many legends have grown up around his name. Some of them are told in the medieval *Golden Legend* which is a compilation of the lives of the saints. It is in this book that the story appears of Nicholas secretly giving bags of gold to the three daughters of a poor neighbor. When Clement C. Moore wrote "A Visit from Saint Nicholas" in New York in 1822, reindeer and sleigh and stockings at the chimney entered into his poem about "St. Nick," but the designation Santa Claus was not used by him. In a more general way gifts borne by Santa Claus symbolize the original gifts of the Wise Men to the Christ Child.

See GIFT, PACK, REINDEER.

Savior

This title of Christ at Christmas comes principally from the message of the herald angel to the shepherds: "To you is born this day in the city of David a Savior who is Christ the Lord," (Luke 2:11). Joseph had a dream in which an angel appeared to him to announce that his wife Mary would bear a son, "and you shall call his name Jesus, for he will save his people from their sins" (Matthew 1:21). The Jewish nation was also looking for a savior king who should set them free from foreign yoke.

Scepter (Sceptre)

As an emblem of royal power and au-thority kings may hold a rod or wand called a scepter. Originally this may have been simply a staff and later a weapon. Scepters frequently terminate at the top with a further symbol such as an eagle. To show that they represent the sovereign God angels may hold a scepter. In Annunciation scenes Gabriel sometimes carries one as the herald of God. The symbol of the scepter is used in a famous messianic passage in the Old Testament, Numbers 24:17, "A scepter shall rise out of Israel."

Sheep and Shepherds

The shepherds "in the field keeping watch over their flock by night" represent the humble Jewish folk to whom Christ was first presented. They may be contrasted with the foreign, non-Jewish (Gentile) Magi who came from distant lands bearing rich gifts. One tradition places their sheep field at the "tower of the flock" which is near Rachel's tomb on the road from Bethlehem to Jerusalem.

Shell

The scallop shell with a few drops of water is a symbol of baptism, and at times of the Baptism of Christ. In this latter scene it is held by John the Baptist.

Stable

What sort of a shelter was Mary in when Jesus was born? The Gospels do

 not say. The idea of a stable is suggested by Luke's manger and "no place for them in the inn." It could have been a one-room Palestinian cottage in which domestic animals shared space with the family. Matthew refers to the "house" in which the Magi found the Holy Family.

The tradition that the holy birth took place in a cave seems to have originated in the middle of the second century A.D. Several of the apocryphal gospels mention it. The latest one (Gospel of Pseudo-Matthew) tells us that Mary took her baby from the cave into a stable on the third day. *The Golden Legend* cites an authority to show that Joseph and Mary found shelter in a shed between two houses. Cave, stable, shed—all appear in one or another of the paintings, sculptures or crèche scenes.

Usually the shed or stable is depicted as being a rather open shelter; sometimes a building falling into ruins. The humble beginning of the Savior's life is thus vividly brought to mind. We can also recall Christ's words to would-be disciples: "Foxes have holes, and birds of the air have nests; but the Son of Man has nowhere to lay his head" (Matthew 8:20).

See CAVE, CRIB, ASS, OX.

Star

The star is one of a number of royal symbols. By Christian times it had become a messianic symbol as well. In addition to the appearance of the star to the Magi recorded in Matthew 2:2, we find an oracle in Numbers 24:17, "a star shall come forth out of Jacob," used by Christians as a prediction of Christ; and in Revelation 22:16 the heavenly Jesus said, "I am the root and offspring of David, the bright morning star."

The Star of the East, which the Wise Men from the East followed to Bethlehem, is both a symbol of the "king of the Jews" and a sign of divine guidance to that King. As Persians the Magi probably believed that this star was the *fravashi* of a great man, that is, the heavenly image or prototype. Medieval artists started the custom of placing the face of a child  or an angel in a bright disk in the sky to represent this star. The second century apocryphal Gospel of the Infancy by Thomas (III. 3) records, "at the same time there appeared to them an angel in the form of that star which had before been their guide in their journey." Medieval artists certainly knew that the *Golden Legend* told that according to Chrysostom the Magi saw a star which had the shape of a child with a fiery cross on his head.

The Star of Bethlehem is five-pointed. It is properly an Epiphany rather than a Christmas symbol.

Sun of Righteousness

"The sun of righteousness shall rise, with healing in its wings," is a reference in Malachi 4:2 to what will happen at the day of judgment. The title is used by Christians as a title for Jesus, the Messiah. The sun of God's righteousness symbolizes health and defense. The "wings" are the sun's rays. The winged sun is a symbol in the Near East for blessing and protection.

Torch

All ancient sources of light such as a candle, a lantern, or a torch are appropriate symbols at the Nativity of Christ, the Light of the World. Torches and lanterns also remind us of the traditional idea that Christ was born at midnight.

Tower

The tower of some Nativity scenes may have been suggested by the "tower of the flock" (Migdal-eder) which is near Bethlehem to the east. Micah's prediction (4:8) that the kingdom of the daughter of Jerusalem was to come to the "tower of the flock" was understood as referring to the announcement of the birth of the Messiah. According to this tradition the Shepherds heard the angel's proclamation at this place.

Tree of Jesse (See JESSE TREE)

Tree Ornaments

Christmas tree ornaments may have had their origin in the trimmings of the old Roman Kalends of January celebration. Originally the tree ornaments were substitutes for natural fruit such as apples. The small fruits and nuts used on wreaths today are examples of this an-cient custom of using the bountiful gifts of nature for festival decoration. They symbolize Christmas as a feast. See CHRISTMAS TREE.

Trumpet

The Jews used trumpets in the temple especially at festivals. For instance, the Jewish New Year was announced by the sound of the trumpet. Christians are more likely to picture the trumpet in the hands of an angel than a man. In this case it may be part of the choir of the heavenly host or summoning the elect to the last judgment.

Unicorn

This mythical animal had one horn in the middle of its forehead. According to legend the only way to capture a unicorn was to lay a trap for it, which would be a virgin seated where the unicorn was acccustomed to run. The unicorn would stop and go to her and lay its head in her lap. Christian writers made this an allegory of the Annunciation to the Virgin and the Incarnation of Christ, born of a Virgin.

Wassail and Wassailing

In old England there used to be a Christmas custom of drinking to fruit trees (or to cattle) in order to insure their thriving. Later the custom became a matter of drinking healths from a wassail bowl. Wassailing was the term eventually applied to going about from one house to another at Christmas singing a song of good wishes for Christmas and the New Year. A wassail bowl is filled with spiced ale or beer, which is served foaming hot with apples floating in it.

Wheat

Either a sheaf of wheat or several stalks of wheat appear in some Nativity scenes. These may be intended as food for the animals, or when the shepherds are shown, an offering which they brought. Beyond this, the wheat, which is a familiar ingredient of bread, stands for Jesus who said, "I am the bread of life" (John 6:35) and "the bread of God is that which comes down from heaven, and gives life to the world" (John 6:33).

Wreath

The evergreen wreath, a carryover from paganism, symbolizes victory or immortality. It is frequently seen carved on sarcophagi and tombs. The wreath made of actual leafy boughs is thought to bring to the user the divine power of the tree of life. Furthermore it may represent the presence of divine royalty. See HOLLY, LAUREL.

Yule

This is a Teutonic name for Christmas. Originally Yule was a season roughly equivalent to the months of December and January. On becoming Christians the Germanic tribes kept the name Yule and some of its customs for their observance of Christmas tide. The boar's head and Yule log of the old-time Christmas are two of the Yule survivals.

Lent

As a season Lent was originally a period of preparation for Easter baptism. During this time of instruction the catechumens fasted and prayed. The climax came in the all-night vigil of Easter Even with baptism and confirmation and the celebration of Christ's Resurrection. At a later time all church members joined in making Lent a penitential season of mourning for sin. As time went on more interest was shown in the trials and sufferings of Jesus than in anticipating his victorious Resurrection.

The forty weekdays of Lent represent the period which Jesus spent in the wilderness during his Temptation. According to Matthew and Luke he fasted for forty days. The symbolism of Lent, aside from Holy Week, centers on sin, temptation and penitence. Lent's liturgical color, violet, stands for penitence.

Ashes, Ash Wednesday

The name of the first day of Lent, Ash Wednesday, comes from the old custom of blessing ashes and marking the foreheads of the penitent faithful with ashes on this day. The ashes are prepared by burning palms from the preceding Palm Sunday. This marking is done as a symbol of the penitential character of the Lenten season. The idea comes from Old Testament times when mourners or penitents clothed themselves in sackcloth and sprinkled their heads and faces with dust or ashes. Job said, "Therefore I despise myself and repent in dust and ashes" (Job 42:6). Words of Jesus that apply may be found in Matthew 11:21, "Woe to you, Bethsaida! for if the mighty works done in you had been done in Tyre and Siden, they would have repented long ago in sackcloth and ashes."

But Jesus condemned the hypocrites of his day who made such a display of their piety rather than serving God with the spiritual purpose that should accompany any outward sign of penitence. This is referred to in the following portion of the Ash Wednesday gospel: "When you fast, do not look dismal, like the hypocrites, for they disfigure their faces that their fasting may be seen of men . . . But when you fast, anoint your head and wash your face, that your fasting may not be seen by men but by your Father who is in secret" (Matthew 6:16-18).

Devil, Satan

Because of his role as the tempter the devil comes into prominence during Lent. He is the personification of evil and the mythical enemy of Christ himself as well as of every follower of Christ. Mark (1:13) says that Jesus "was in the wilderness forty days, tempted by Satan." Matthew (4:1) and Luke (4:2) both tell that in the wilderness Jesus was "tempted by the devil," and reveal three temptations which Jesus successfully resisted.

The devil is familiarly depicted as the Prince of the Underworld equipped with a pitchfork. In pictures of Jesus' temptations he often appears with the wings of a fallen angel. He may wear a crown as the King of Pride. Pictorially he is sometimes related to the mythical satyr of unsavory repute and is given the horns and hoofs of a goat.

Revelation 12 contains a vision of the conflict between Christ and Satan. In verse 9 we read "the great dragon was thrown down, that ancient serpent, who is called the Devil and Satan." Accordingly the devil is often represented by a dragon (especially when shown vanquished by St. Michael) or a serpent, or if shown like a man he has a reptile's tail.

The following animals are sometimes used to represent the devil.

Ape, which is also a symbol of sin and lust.

Blackbird, because of its black feathers representing the darkness of sin, and its melodious song, which reminds us of the alluring temptations of the flesh.

Fox, renowned for its cunning and its ability to feign death to attract the unwary.

Leopard, a symbol of sin and cruelty.

Lion, because of its pride and fierceness. This is only one of several different symbolic ideas about this beast. (See LION in Easter section.) Sculptors have represented Christ as standing on a lion, after the idea in Ps. 91:13, "You will tread on the lion and the adder, the young lion and the serpent you will trample under foot."

Owl likes to hide in darkness. It tricks other birds.

Raven, because of its blackness, sometimes represents sin.

Spider, which prepares a trap for the unwary with its web.

Wolf prowls around sheepfolds and is an enemy of the sheep.

In color the devil may be black since that is the traditional appearance of demons; or red because his home is in hell-fire; or green because that is frequently seen in snakes.

Fasting

The Lenten fast was suggested by Jesus' fasting forty days in the wilderness following his baptism. Fasting (which is usually abstinence from food) and other forms of abstinence are used at this time as a sign of subduing the flesh to the spirit and as a sign of penitence.

Holy Week

Holy Week, a subseason of Lent, begins on Palm Sunday (sixth Sunday in Lent) and embraces the last seven days before Easter. The gospel story of Jesus' trial and sufferings, which is usually read in churches on Palm Sunday, is called the Passion, according to St. Matthew, St. Mark or St. Luke. The gospel Passion story includes, in one gospel or another, the agony in Gethsemane, the betrayal and arrest, the hearings before the High Priest and Herod, the trial under Pontius Pilate, the scourging and mocking of Jesus by the soldiers, carrying the cross to Calvary, and the crucifixion and death of Jesus.

The cross is often used as a seasonal symbol for Lent and for Holy Week.

Holy Week symbolism naturally centers on the Instruments of the Passion and on persons and things mentioned in the gospel accounts of the Crucifixion. Again, as at Christmas-Epiphany, legend has added much which is not explicit in the Bible accounts.

Basin and Ewer (Pitcher)

The washing of hands with water symbolizes innocence. Pilate publicly washed his hands after Jesus' trial. "So when Pilate saw that he was gaining nothing, but rather that a riot was beginning, he took water and washed his hands before the crowd, saying, 'I am innocent of this man's blood'" (Matthew 27:24).

Calvary (See GOLGOTHA)

Centurion

This Roman army officer had charge of the soldiers who carried out the Crucifixion. Some artists make him, a Gentile, stand for the Church on the basis of his words at Christ's death, "Truly this man was the Son of God!" (Mark 15:39 KJV). To correspond with this symbolism of the Church the same artists depicted the Jewish man with the sponge of vinegar as the Synagogue.

Cock

This is a symbol of Peter's denial and so one of the symbols of the Passion. After Peter had asserted his loyalty, "Jesus said to him, 'Truly, I say to you, this very night, before the cock crows, you will deny me three times'" (Matthew 26:34). "Before the cock crows" was a proverbial way of indicating early in the morning.

Coins

Thirty silver coins was the price of the betrayal of Christ by Judas Iscariot and thus it becomes one of the symbols of the Passion. Judas went to the chief priests "and said, 'What will you give me if I deliver him to you?' And they paid him thirty pieces of silver" (Matthew 26:15). "When Judas, his betrayer, saw that he was condemned, he repented and brought back the thirty pieces of silver to the chief priests and the elders, saying, 'I have sinned in betraying innocent blood'" (Matthew 27:3-4). See also PURSE.

Cross

The Golden Legend has preserved the apocryphal story of the connection of the wood of the cross with the Tree of Knowledge in the Garden of Eden. Briefly put, the legend tells that a branch of this tree was planted on Adam's grave. Solomon had it cut down to use in building the temple, but it was found unsuitable. Instead it was used for a time as a bridge across a brook. Later it was buried in the Pool of Bethesda. At the time of the Crucifixion it floated up and was used for the wood of the cross.

The cross is a symbol of Christ because of his sacrifice on it. It is also a symbol of Christianity. Theologically it stands for salvation, redemption and atonement.

The Latin cross (four arms with the lower one twice as long) is the traditional form used for the Crucifixion and the Atonement. See also CROSS in the Feasts of the Pentecost Season section.

Crown of Thorns

The crown of thorns placed on Christ's head by the soldiers in derision symbolizes the Passion and the Crucifixion. It stands for a royal diadem and the reed stands for a king's scepter. "And plaiting a crown of thorns they put it on his head, and put a reed in his right hand. And kneeling before him they mocked him, saying, 'Hail, King of the Jews!'" (Matthew 27:29). In pictures Christ usually wears this crown of thorns until taken down from the cross. When used as a separate symbol it is often accompanied by the three nails.

Crucifixion Scene

During the Middle Ages a great deal of symbolism came into use in connection with the Crucifixion. Some of these are noted under this title.

1. *The new Eve and the Church*. This symbolism is connected with the wound in Christ's side made by the soldier (John 19:34), and with the concept of Christ as the new or second Adam. Paul had written: "For as in Adam all die, so also in Christ shall all be made alive" (I Corinthians 15:22). As Eve came out of the side of Adam, so the Church came from the wounded side of Christ. The blood and water which gushed out from the wound are symbols of the two chief sacraments, Baptism and the Eucharist. The new Eve, the Church, is sometimes shown beside the wound receiving the blood and water in her chalice.

2. Symbolic figures which may be seen in representations of the Crucifixion are (explained individually elsewhere in this section): CROWN OF THORNS, I.N.R.I., SPEAR, SPONGE, SKULL AND BONES, SUN AND MOON, INSTRUMENTS OF THE PASSION.

3. Some of the following persons are often shown at the Cross: Two criminals on crosses, one on each side of Christ. They were condemned to be crucified with him (Matthew 27:38ff; Mark 15:27ff; Luke 23:39ff).

St. John, the beloved disciple (John 19:26).

The Roman centurion who said. "This man was a son of God." (Matthew 27:54; Mark 15:39; Luke 23:47).

Some of the women who had followed Jesus from Galilee:

The Virgin Mary, Mary Magdalene, Mary wife of Clopas (John 19:25).

Mary Magdalene, Mary mother of James, Salome (Mark 15:40).

Mary Magdalene, Mary mother of James, mother of sons of Zebedee (James and John) (Matthew 27:56).

Cup

The cup sometimes shown with Jesus while he was praying in Gethsemane is a symbol of the Agony in the Garden. Usually it is held by an angel. This cup is a figure  of speech in the Gethsemane prayer: "My Father, if it be possible, let this cup pass from me; nevertheless, not as I will, but as thou wilt" (Matthew 26:39). This cup is the cup of suffering. Jesus knew that the supreme sacrifice on the cross could not be far away.

Dandelion

Early paintings of the Crucifixion sometimes show this bitter herb as a symbol of the passion.

Dice

Two or three dice along with the seamless robe of Christ have become Passion symbols because the soldiers cast lots for his garments. "And they crucified him, and divided his garments among them, casting lots for them, to decide what each should take" (Mark 15:24). A precedent was found in Psalms 22:18,

> "they divide my garments among them,
> and for my raiment they cast lots."

Eagle Standard

A silver or bronze eagle on a standard was a military symbol serving as an ensign of Roman legions. This is sometimes shown in pictures of various Passion scenes.

Gall

"They offered him wine to drink, mingled with gall" (Matthew 27:34). Gall is a bitter liquid. Mark refers to myrrh at this point. Jesus refused this drug which would have acted as an opiate and would have reduced the pain of the crucifixion. He preferred to remain fully conscious and to bear his suffering with courage.

Gethsemane

The "Garden" of Gethsemane was the scene of the Agony in the Garden and the Betrayal. Three disciples are often shown with Jesus in Gethsemane. They are Peter, James and John. In some scenes they are shown asleep. "And he came to the disciples and found them sleeping . . ." (Matthew 26:40). The term "agony" comes from Luke as does the figure of an angel. "And there appeared to him an angel from heaven, strengthening him. And being in an agony he prayed more earnestly; and his sweat became like great drops of blood falling down upon the ground" (Luke 22:43-44).

Goldfinch

Because of its fondness for eating thistles and thorns, which are a reminder of the crown of thorns, the goldfinch is a symbol of the Passion.

Golgotha or Calvary

The name Golgotha is used in the Gospels for the place of crucifixion outside the wall of Jerusalem. This Hebrew word means "skull." Calvary refers to the same place, but is taken from the Latin word for skull. Some pictures of the Crucifixion show a skull for this reason and also because a legend exists that this is where Adam was buried and the skull is his.

In the Middle Ages some people maintained that on this spot Adam was created out of the dust of the ground, that here Mary received from the angel the annunciation of her bearing Jesus the Savior, that Adam was buried here and that Jesus' blood flowed over Adam's bones. See SKULL AND BONES.

Good Friday

The "good" part is an old expression for holy. Friday is the traditional day of the week not only for the Crucifixion but also for the creation of Adam, the fall of Adam, the death of Abel, and the Annunciation.

Grapes and Wheat

A bunch of grapes and several ears of wheat (sometimes with a chalice) make a symbol of the Last Supper or of the Holy Eucharist. The grape, like the wine of communion, represents the Blood of Christ, following his words at the Last Supper, "This is my blood," which he said when he gave them the cup. The flour of wheat is a usual ingredient of bread. Jesus said of the bread, "This is my body."

Hammer

Although not mentioned in Scripture, the use of a hammer for nailing Christ to the cross is assumed. So it is symbolic of the Crucifixion and is one of the instruments of the Passion.

I. N. R. I.

This symbol placed on a board at the top of the cross stands for the initial letters of four Latin words, *"Iesus Nazarenus Rex Iudaeorum"* ("Jesus of Nazareth King of the Jews"). "Pilate also wrote a title and put it on the cross; it read, 'Jesus of Nazareth, the King of the Jews.' . . . and it was written in Hebrew, in Latin, and in Greek" (John 19:19-20). This trilingual inscription signified for John the evangelist the universal mission of Christ. Originally in art the inscription, if used at all, was written out in full. Italian artists in the thirteenth century cut this down to the familiar abbreviation. Since each of these letters is an initial of a word, it is proper to put a period after each.

Instruments of the Passion

A number of symbols are known by tradition as Instruments of the Passion. They will rarely all be found in one piece of art, but several of them will usually be seen in the various representations of Jesus on the cross. See items: BASIN AND EWER, COCK, COINS, CROWN OF THORNS, DICE, HAMMER, LADDER, LANTERN, NAILS, PILLAR, PINCERS, REED, ROBE, SKULL, SPEAR, SPONGE.

Joseph of Arimathea

Joseph, a member of the Sanhedrin and a secret disciple of Jesus, asked Pilate for the body and took care of the Burial of Jesus. He is usually shown in scenes of the Deposition and the Entombment (see Mark 15: 42-47.)

Ladder

This unscriptural symbol belongs with the Instruments of the Passion. In scenes of the Descent from the Cross it frequently appears. Joseph of Arimathea or Nicodemus may be shown climbing the ladder to remove the nails.

Lamb

The title "Lamb of God" (lamb provided by God) was given Jesus by John the Baptist (John 1:29,36). The symbolism goes back to Isaiah 53:7, "like a lamb that is led to the slaughter," where the lamb is a type of vicarious suffering. The Paschal lamb eaten at Passover was a symbol of God's deliverance of his people. The cross-bearing lamb stands for Christ crucified. Sometimes blood flows from the lamb's breast into a chalice in imitation of the wound in Christ's side from which flowed blood and water. John 19:34-36 refers to this and quotes from Exodus 12:46 which is about the Passover lamb. See JOHN THE BAPTIST in Christmas section.

Lanterns and Torches

These are emblems of the Betrayal and the Passion, referring to the arrest of Jesus by night in Gethsemane. "So Judas, procuring a band of soldiers and some officers from the chief priests and the Pharisees, went there with lanterns and torches and weapons" (John 18:3).

Man of Sorrows

This term for Christ, which is used to describe the Christ of the Passion showing his five wounds, comes from Isaiah 53:3,

"He was despised and rejected by men;
a man of sorrows, and acquainted with grief."

The whole chapter is frequently read in Good Friday church services as a prediction of the Passion.

Maundy Thursday

The Church remembers the institution of the Lord's Supper on this day.

"Maundy" is derived from the Latin *mandatum*, or commandment, which is found as the first word in Latin of John 13:34, "A new commandment I give you, that you love one another." This verse is an antiphon from the ceremony of foot-washing done on this day in imitation of Jesus washing the feet of his disciples just before the Last Supper (see John 13:1-15).

Nails

The use of nails in crucifying Christ is based on the request of Thomas after the

Resurrection to see the print of the nails in Jesus' hands (John 20:25). Three nails are a symbol of the Passion (often shown with the crown of thorns). Early crucifixes placed the feet side by side and used four nails, but by the thirteenth century the number was reduced to three, one nail sufficing for both feet.

Nicodemus

Mentioned only in the Gospel of John, Nicodemus, who like Joseph of Arimathea was a member of the Sanhedrin, brought myrrh and aloes for the Burial of Jesus and assisted in placing the body in the tomb. He is frequently shown in scenes of the Entombment.

Owl

In the scenes of the Crucifixion the owl symbolizes darkness and solitude as an attribute of Christ. The allusion is to a verse in Psalm 102:6, "I am like a pelican in the wilderness: I am like an owl of the desert" (King James Version).

Palm Branches

"Branches of palm trees" are used as symbols of the Triumphal Entry into Jerusalem on Palm Sunday, following the account in John 12:12-14. The palm is a symbol of victory. The Jews used palm and willow branches in observing the Feast of Booths or Tabernacles (see Leviticus 23:40).

Passover

This Jewish spring festival is the time when Jesus Christ ate the Last Supper with his disciples and the next morning was crucified. The first three Gospels leave the impression that the Last Supper was also the Passover meal, but John's Gospel places the Supper on the Day of Preparation (Jewish days began at sundown) and makes the Crucifixion and Christ's death occur at the time when the paschal lambs were being sacrificed.

The Passover was a memorial of the deliverance of the Hebrew people from slavery in Egypt. The blood of the lamb which was killed for the original Passover

was put on the lintels and posts of the doors of houses where the people of Israel dwelt. This served as a signal to the "destroyer" to pass over these homes on

45

his errand to slay the first-born of the Egyptians. The full story is recounted in Exodus 12.

The word "paschal" comes from the Hebrew name of Passover, *Pesach*.

Pelican

A legend popular with early Christian writers is responsible for finding in this bird an emblem of self-sacrifice. According to the story the pelican saves the life of its young by stabbing its breast with its beak and sprinkling them with its own blood. One version tells that the young are killed by a serpent and restored to life after three days. Thus this bird symbolizes Christ's sacrifice on the Cross and the shedding of his blood for the love of mankind.

Psalm 102:6 reads in the Septuagint and in the King James Version, "I am like a pelican of the wilderness: I am like an owl of the desert." This was accepted as an allusion to Christ in the loneliness of his Passion.

Pillar

The pillar was a necessary adjunct to the scourging of Jesus and therefore is an emblem of the Passion. Cords used in the scourging or in tying Jesus to the column are also shown sometimes.

Purse

The purse of Judas, a symbol of the Betrayal, is sometimes shown with the thirty silver pieces paid by the chief priests to Judas. See COINS.

Redeemer

While this word does not occur in the New Testament and is an Old Testament term, it is nevertheless often applied to Jesus Christ in connection with his death on the Cross. In Isaiah 41:14 the Lord says, "Your Redeemer is the Holy  One of Israel." God is here the liberator of his people. The redeemer buys the freedom of a slave by paying his ransom and this idea of redemption is one that is found in the New Testament. Jesus said, "For the son of man also came not to be served but to serve, and to give his life as a ransom for many" (Mark 10:45).

Reed

On the cross Christ was offered a sponge filled with vinegar on the end of a reed (Matthew 27:48 and a reference to Psalm 69:21). This is one of the symbols of the Passion. See GALL, SPONGE.

Robe of Christ

Scarlet or purple robe. This robe was put on Jesus by the soldiers while they were mocking him as King of the Jews and is one of the symbols of the Passion. (See Matthew 27:27-31, Mark 15: 16-20).

The Seamless robe is another symbol of the Passion. In some versions it is called a coat, in others a tunic. ". . . But his tunic was without seam, woven from

top to bottom; so they said to one another 'Let us not tear it, but cast lots for it to see whose it shall be'" (John 19:23-24).

Rope

The rope was used by the soldiers to bind Jesus when he was betrayed by Judas in Gethsemane (John 18:12) and again in the morning "they bound him and led him away and delivered him to Pilate the governor" (Matthew 27:2).

Saint John

Crucifixion scenes may show a man and a woman standing on either side of the cross. Jesus' mother has the place of honor on his right, while St. John stands at Jesus' left side. The Gospel of John tells us (19:26-27): "When Jesus saw his mother, and the disciple whom he loved standing near, he said to his mother, 'Woman behold your son!' Then he said to the disciple, 'Behold your mother!'"

Scorpion

The scorpion is a type of spider having a long tail with a poisonous sting. As such it is a symbol of evil and treachery and so of Judas. It may be shown on shields or flags of the soldiers at the Crucifixion.

Scourge

 This is one of the symbols of the Passion. It represents the scourging of Jesus by order of Pilate. A scourge is a kind of a whip with several tails. It was a Roman custom to scourge a prisoner before crucifying him.

Serpent

A serpent shown at the foot of the cross signifies the evil responsible for the Fall of Man and now overcome by the Death of Christ, the Redeemer. A serpent entwined on a cross stands for Christ and his Crucifixion in the sense of John 3:14, "As Moses lifted up the serpent in the wilderness, so must the son of man be lifted up."

Skull and Bones

In Crucifixion scenes the skull at the foot of the Cross, plus some bones, refers to the name of the hill, Golgotha, which means "the place of a skull," and the legend that this was also the burial place of Adam. Christ, the second Adam, redeems men who are handicapped by the Fall of the first Adam. See GOLGOTHA.

Spear

The spear or lance used to pierce the side of Christ while he was on the cross (John 19:34) is one of the Instruments of the Passion. It is often shown with the sponge on a reed.

Sponge

"And one of them at once ran and took a sponge, filled it with vinegar, and put it on a reed, and gave it to him to drink" (Matt. 27:48). This is another Instrument of the Passion. See GALL, REED.

S. P. Q. R.

These initials inscribed on the military standards of Rome sometimes appear in Crucifixion scenes. The Latin *Senatus Populusque Romanus* means "the Senate and People of Rome," an official title of the Roman state.

Sun and Moon

The sun, shining or darkened, and sometimes the moon are shown at the  Crucifixion to symbolize the sympathy of nature with the sufferings of the crucified. The darkened sun is from Luke 23:44-45, "It was now about the sixth hour [noon], and there was darkness over the whole land until the ninth hour, while the sun's light failed [or, the sun was eclipsed] . . ." Jesus had predicted, "the sun will be darkened, and the moon will not give its light" (Matthew 24:29). This is an ancient pagan death symbol.

Thistle

The thistle as a thorny plant and a symbol of sorrow is a symbol of the Passion and in particular the crowning with thorns. The original symbolism comes from the Fall of Adam:

". . . cursed is the ground because of you; in toil you shall eat of it all the days of your life; thorns and thistles it shall bring forth to you . . ." (Genesis 3:17-18)

Torch (See LANTERNS)

Virgin Mary

The fourth Gospel alone mentions the presence of Jesus' mother at the Crucifixion (John 19:25-26), but she is often depicted as standing on her son's right at the cross. During the Middle Ages she was sometimes made in this scene a symbol of the new Eve (corresponding to Jesus Christ the new Adam) or else the Church contrasted with the superseded Synagogue on the left. See CRUCIFIXION SCENE.

Winding Sheet

Jews were often buried in a burial cloth or winding sheet which was wrapped around the body before it was laid in the tomb. These are the "linen cloths" of John 20:4. This sheet may be 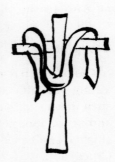 shown in scenes of Jesus' Burial; in some instances the sheet is draped over the arms of the cross as a symbol of the burial.

Easter—Ascension

Eastertide includes the whole period of fifty days starting with Easter Day and concluding on Pentecost. So it commemorates the Resurrection, the Ascension and the descent of the Holy Spirit. The Apostles' Creed says, "On the third day he rose again. He ascended into heaven, and is seated at the right hand of the Father." Acts gives the impression that the Ascension may have occurred "forty days" after the Resurrection. From the tomb Jesus Christ, "the King of Glory," proceeded to his eternal throne where he reigns as King of the Kingdom of God. Traditional thought places the kingly crown on his head, replacing the crown of thorns, at this time. It is also a crown of his victory over death. Hence the crown of the King makes an appropriate symbol for this whole period.

The depicting of the risen Christ may be made more explicit by one or more of these attributes: a white or golden garment, the banner of the Resurrection (appropriate from his rising until his Ascension), the five wounds, a radiance around him. A crucifix on which Christ is shown clad in eucharistic vestments represents the Reigning Christ or Christ the King.

Angel of the Resurrection

The angel or two angels at the empty tomb are mentioned by all four Gospels and are always described as dressed in white. True to their intended function they are messengers from God to men (or in this case to women). The white garments are appropriate to the joy of Christ's Resurrection.

Banner with Cross

The Lamb of God carrying this banner and Christ rising from the grave bearing such a banner are exhibiting a symbol of victory—the victory over death won by Christ.

Butterfly

Because the caterpillar goes into a cocoon (tomb) where it seemingly dies only to emerge as a butterfly, this insect has become a symbol of Christ's Resurrection and the resurrection of all men.

Christ in Limbo (Hell)

An old Christian belief reflected in the Apostles' Creed is that in the time between his Death and his Resurrection Christ descended into limbo, the outer circle of hell reserved for souls who had died previous to Christ's coming on earth. Paintings of this scene show Christ arriving at the gate to the underworld and carrying the symbol of his victory over death which is a banner inscribed with a cross and attached to a staff. As the souls in limbo greet him, Adam is shown as the first man to emerge. This legend is called the Harrowing of Hell ("harrow" in the sense of "rob"). Its literary antecedent is the apocryphal *Gospel of Nicodemus.*

Crown

The use of crowns to denote sovereignty and kingship, or in other cases as wreaths to denote victory, is very ancient. The idea that Jesus Christ received his crown of victory when he ascended has made such a symbol appropriate for both Easter and Ascension. The faithful believer will receive the crown of life at death (Revelation 2:10).

Daniel and Two Lions

The scene of Daniel standing between two lions appears often on Christian sarcophagi and in the catacombs from the earliest days. As Daniel was delivered from being destroyed by the lions (Daniel 6:16-23) so will the Christian be granted deliverance by God in the life to come.

Dolphin

With pagans the dolphin had become a popular symbol of salvation and immortality before Christians took it over for use in the Catacombs. Sometimes used as the fish which swallowed Jonah and cast him forth on the third day, the dolphin easily became symbolic of the Resurrection of Christ. See JONAH.

Eagle

The eagle is one of the four living creatures around the throne of God mentioned in Revelation 4:7, "the first living creature like a lion, the second living creature like an ox, the third living creature with the face of a man, and the fourth living creature like a flying eagle." As early as the second century in addition to being assigned to the four Evangelists, the living creatures were made symbolic of four events in the life of Christ: the Nativity (man), his sacrificial Death (ox), the Resurrection (lion), and the Ascension which is represented by the flying eagle. See also LION in this section.

Easter

Bede gives the origin of this English name for the festival of Christ's Resurrection. He derives the word from the name of a pagan goddess called Eostre (another spelling of Eastre) whose festival came at the spring equinox. Some other modern languages derive their name for Easter from the Latin *pascha,* in turn taken from the Hebrew *pesach* or Passover. This acknowledges that the Christian feast is a successor to the Jewish Passover. The Sunday on which Easter falls each year is determined by when the full moon on or next after March 21 occurs. The Sunday following this full moon is appointed as Easter. This system relates the Resurrection anniversary to the Passover, which was the time of the original Passion of Christ. The date of Easter each year settles the date for Ash Wednesday and Lent, and the length of the season after Pentecost.

Easter Lily

Being a spring flower the Easter lily is a common symbol of the Resurrection. Another reason for this symbolism is the sprouting of a beautiful flower from a seemingly dead bulb which is buried in the ground.

Egg

The egg became a symbol of the Resurrection and of Easter because the chick enclosed in the shell (like a tomb) breaks forth to life. The fertilized egg looks dead but contains the promise of life. Colored eggs represent the gay hues of an Easter sunrise.

Empty Tomb

The actual rising of Christ from the tomb is not described in the Gospels and for many years was not pictured in art. The tomb with the stone rolled away, or a sarcophagus (stone coffin) with cover pushed aside is a symbol of Christ's Resurrection. The sarcophagus type of tomb is, of course, unscriptural. The movable stone of the tomb gave the Church Fathers a chance for further symbolism. They said that it was the table of stone on which was written the Hebrew Law. Christ was hidden beneath that stone. When he rose from the dead the Law no longer had any meaning for his followers.

Gate of Heaven, Gate of Hell

Heaven was sometimes conceived of as a Garden of Paradise. It was entered through a gate by Christ at his Resurrection and Ascension.

According to the Apostles' Creed Christ descended into hell before rising to heaven. This is based on I Peter 3:19, "he went and preached to the spirits in prison." Representations of Christ's Descent into Hell show him breaking through the gate of hell and trampling the fragments with his feet. See CHRIST IN LIMBO.

Gourd (See JONAH)

Hare, Rabbit

The "Easter bunny" is not a true Christian symbol. The hare or rabbit is a symbol of fertility and therefore of life predominant over death.

Ivy

Because of its lasting greenness, ivy serves as a symbol of immortality and eternal life.

Jonah

Two incidents in the story of Jonah have been connected with the Resurrection since the time of the Roman catacombs: Jonah and the whale, and Jonah under the gourd.

Jonah 1:17 says that "The Lord appointed a great fish to swallow up Jonah; and Jonah was in the belly of the fish three days and three nights." Jesus said, "For as Jonah was three days and three nights in the belly of the whale, so will the Son of man be three days and three nights in the heart of the earth" (Matthew 12:40). In some cases Jonah is shown diving into the sea, or, more according to the Bible, being thrown overboard. But in other cases the "resurrection" of Jonah appears as he is cast forth by the whale.

The final scene in the story (Jonah 4:6) shows the prophet reclining under an arbor of ivy or under a gourd plant. Jerome, perhaps bending to an artistic tradition, translated the plant as "ivy." Augustine preferred the more correct word "gourd." (Bible scholars guess it was a castor oil plant.) The artists indicate that Jonah was enjoying everlasting bliss (omitting the worm and the withering of 4:7).

The early artists usually represented the "great fish" as a sea monster or a dolphin.

Lamb with Banner

The standing lamb bearing the cross-emblazoned banner of victory signifies the Resurrection.

Representing Jesus the Son of God, the lamb has a three-rayed nimbus around his head. The banner is a swallow-tailed pennon and the staff has a cross top.

"At the Lamb's high feast we sing," an Easter hymn (originally in the Latin

Breviary) emphasizes the origin of this symbol in the paschal lamb. Two lines in the original English version read:

"Now thy banner thou dost wave;
Vanquished Satan and the grave."

Lion

This very old symbol is associated with many different ideas, but one of the chief of them is the Resurrection. Gregory the Great (about 600 A.D.) is responsible for taking over the fabulous natural history of the lion current in his day and associating it with Christ's Resurrection. Two actions of the lion were impressive. Popularly he was supposed to sleep with his eyes open: "Behold, he who keeps Israel will neither slumber nor sleep" (Psalm 121:4). Furthermore it was reported that lion cubs were born dead and after three days their father breathed or roared over them and they came to life.

Also the power of the lion is impressive. Said Gregory: "He himself is . . . a lion because by the strength of his Godhead he burst the band of the death he had undergone." This is included in a passage likening Christ to the four living creatures of Ezekiel. For another symbolic use of the lion, read the article on EAGLE in this section.

Pasch, Paschal

Derived from the Latin and Greek *Pascha* which in turn comes from the Hebrew *Pesach*, these words referred originally to the Passover, but were taken over by Christians to designate Easter which first occurred in connection with the Passover. The Paschal lamb was the lamb without blemish commanded to be slain and eaten by the Jews at Passover (Exodus 12:1-13). Jesus Christ, who died at Passover, is often called the Paschal Lamb, or Paschal victim. The Easter Latin hymn *"Victimae paschali laudes,"* translated as "Christians to the Paschal victim, Offer your thankful praises," makes use of this symbol. From this hymn in the Middle Ages the first liturgical dramas were developed for use at Easter. Thus the *"Victimae paschali"* is the origin of the modern Easter story-play.

Paschal Candle

 In ancient usage this Easter candle was lit on Easter Eve and burned at services until Ascension Day. With the revision of the church calendar, it is now customary that the paschal candle burn at all services through the Day of Pentecost, which is the new termination of the Easter season. The paschal candlestick stands at the gospel side of the altar. This candle symbolizes Christ the Light who has overcome the darkness of the world.

Peacock

This symbol of immortality was taken over from the Romans by the early Christians. According to a medieval bestiary the peacock's "flesh is so hard that it is scarcely subject to putrefaction." St. Augustine (in his *City of God*) remarked, "Who except God, the Creator of all things, endowed the flesh of the dead peacock with the power of never decaying?"

Phoenix

A mythical bird of reddish-purple color (from *phoeniceus* or "purple") provided the early Christians with a very popular symbol to be used on burial stones and in writing as a sign of the Resurrection. Briefly put, the legend tells of a bird that lives for five hundred years, builds a nest for a funeral pyre and burns itself to death. Then it rises from its own ashes and starts a new life.

Herodotus, the Greek historian, got the story from Egypt where they said that the bird came from Arabia and sacrificed itself on the altar of the sun. Pliny, a Roman writer, tells the story too. Christian writers took it over, the first known to do so being Clement of Rome about 98 A.D. He gives the legend in his Letter to the Corinthians and makes it an example of the Creator of the universe bringing about the resurrection of the faithful. Later the phoenix signified the Resurrection of Christ.

There are two versions of the legend. One explains that the phoenix flies to the altar of the sun at Heliopolis and burns itself to ashes. From the ashes a little worm survives, next day changes to a bird, and on the third day flies away to Arabia. The other  version tells that the bird builds a nest ("coffin," the ancient accounts read) of spices. This is set on fire by the heat of the sun. The phoenix remains there, fanning the flames with its wings. From the corpse a worm emerges and grows into a new phoenix.

Pomegranate

This fruit (the name means "apple having many seeds") is native to the Bible lands and is mentioned several times in the Old Testament. The fruit was used as a sacred symbol in ancient times. Because of its many seeds the pomegranate became an emblem of fertility and life. When it is used as a symbol of immortality and resurrection, it is shown bursting open to expose the seeds. Thus it is a reminder of Christ bursting open his tomb.

The pomegranate was used as a symbol in ancient pagan religions. It is connected with Demeter (Ceres) and with her daughter Persephone (Proserpine). For her story see POMEGRANATE in the Christmas section.

Swallow

People used to be puzzled as to what happened to the summer swallow in winter. Actually it migrates to lands near the equator, but it was thought that the birds hibernated in  the mud and came out again in spring as if reborn. This led to the use of this bird as a symbol of resurrection. It is also a bird which, among others such as the dove and eagle, was regarded by the ancients as carrying the soul to heaven.

See also INCARNATION in the Christmas-Epiphany section.

Pentecost

The Christian Festival of Pentecost is based on the incident recounted in Acts 2 when the Holy Spirit came upon the Christian disciples gathered in a house at Jerusalem seven weeks after Easter. The appearance was made known by a sound "like the rush of a mighty wind" and by a light in the form of tongues "as of fire, distributed and resting on each of them" (Acts 2:1-3). The Jewish Pentecost which the disciples were celebrating at the time was the Feast of Weeks, a thanksgiving for the first fruits of the wheat harvest (Exodus 34:22). Later Christians in their worship for this week also remembered, by reading Numbers 11:24-30, the incident of the Spirit resting upon the seventy elders of Israel when they were in the wilderness with Moses.

Symbols appropriate to Pentecost are those indicating the appearance of God and his Holy Spirit. Chief among these is the dove. Red is the liturgical color used for the Day of Pentecost and it symbolizes the flames of fire seen at the time of the descent of the Holy Spirit on the disciples in Jerusalem.

Counselor (Comforter)

"Counselor" is the term used of the Holy Spirit by Jesus in the Gospel of John (John 14:16, 16:7), meaning one called to stand by one's side in adversity. In the King James Bible the same Greek word, *Parakletos*, is translated as Comforter (in the Latin sense of "Strengthener"). The Holy Spirit came at Pentecost to help and advise the disciples.

Dove

The usual symbol of the Holy Spirit is the dove descending, always with the three-rayed nimbus which indicates divinity. In a more general sense the dove indicates the power of God at work in men.

Paraclete

This is the English form of the Greek title *Parakletos* or Counselor, referring to the Holy Spirit.

Pentecost

The word "Pentecost," used for both the Jewish and the Christian festival (formerly Christian Whitsunday), means "fiftieth (day)" from the Passover. Counting the Sundays at each end of seven weeks, it is the fiftieth day from Easter. The Jewish festival was originally known as the Feast of Weeks and honored the beginning of the wheat harvest. Later it became a commemoration of the giving of the Law (Ten Commandments) at Mt. Sinai.

Seven Doves

Seven doves arranged around a circle symbolize the seven gifts of the Spirit as listed in Isaiah 11:2—wisdom, understanding, counsel, might, knowledge, fear of the Lord—plus piety, a seventh gift added by the Septuagint version. Within the circle are sometimes found the two capital letters SS, abbreviations for *Sanctus Spiritus*, Latin for Holy Spirit.

Tongues of Flame

This symbol of the Holy Spirit at Pentecost may be in the form of separate flames on the head of each disciple or an overall arrangement of seven tongues together. Fire is an ancient symbol of the divine appearance. God appeared to Moses in the burning bush (Exodus 3:2) and again in the fire and smoke on Mt. Sinai (Exodus 19:18).

Whitsunday

Whitsunday is another name for the Christian festival of Pentecost. This title is generally considered to be a rendering of "White Sunday" from its connection with the white robes worn by the newly baptized at this time. In medieval days when baptism was often done by immersion Pentecost became a popular time for baptism in northern Europe, where the weather might still be cold at Easter.

Feasts of the Pentecost Season

The season immediately following Pentecost comprises 24 to 29 Sundays, the number depending on the date of Easter. The First Sunday after Pentecost is always Trinity Sunday. The whole six-month period of June through November is a time of growing and harvesting crops. Green, its liturgical color, thus represents the growth and luxuriance in nature which is characteristic of this season in northern climates.

For several centuries the Sundays in this period were termed Sundays after Trinity in Anglican and Episcopal churches, but the Roman Catholic Church has always retained the Sundays after Pentecost designation. The American Episcopal Church in its new Prayer Book has reverted to the original nomenclature.

Symbols which can appropriately be used in this season belong mostly to the several special days and the arrangement here accordingly has reference to these days as they come in the calendar.

TRINITY SUNDAY
TRANSFIGURATION
HOLY CROSS DAY
ALL SAINTS

Trinity Sunday, the Sunday after Pentecost

Christian theology interprets the Christian God as being revealed to man in three "persons" or forms: Father, Son, and Holy Spirit. Trinity Sunday 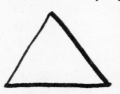 honors this doctrine. Since God is one God—and not three gods—some of the Trinity symbols emphasize this, but some painters years ago delighted in showing the Trinity as three persons in the forms of an old man (the Father) above all, the Son Jesus (usually on the cross) below him, and a dove to indicate the Spirit. A few pictures of the Annunciation to the Virgin show the Father seated in heaven and the dove on the way down to Mary.

A common symbol for Trinity Sunday is the equilateral triangle. In this section Part I will be devoted to symbols of God as the Trinity, and Parts II, III, and IV to the different persons of the Trinity.

I. THE TRINITY

Clover or Shamrock

The three-leaved clover (three leaves on one stem) makes a good Trinity symbol. Legend says that when St. Patrick was preaching to pagans in Ireland he picked up a shamrock as an illustration of the Trinity.

Eye

The all-seeing eye of God displayed within a triangle is properly a symbol of the Trinity. Usually it has rays emanating from each of the three sides of the triangle. A possible source of this idea is the verse in Proverbs 15:3,

"The eyes of the Lord are in every place keeping watch on the evil and on the good."

Fleur-de-Lis

Although more frequently used as a symbol of the Virgin Mary, the fleur-de-lis, because of its trident appearance, is also a symbol of the Trinity. Sometimes it is used as the terminus of the arms of the cross. The fleur-de-lis is a heraldic device representing an iris or lily.

Holy, Holy, Holy

The word "holy" repeated three times stands for the Holy Trinity. The threefold holy is used in hymns and is often employed as a symbol on altars. The Christian use of this symbol comes from Revelation 4:8,

"Holy, holy, holy, is the Lord God Almighty, who was and is and is to come!"

This is the song of the four living creatures around the throne of God (see EAGLE in the Easter section). But ultimately the source of the three holies is Isaiah 6:3, where the seraphim repeat "holy" three times for emphasis.

Shield of the Holy Trinity

This is a triangular diagram, with words originally in Latin, but also seen in modern versions with English words. In the middle is a circle enclosing the word *Deus* or God. At the two top cor-

his raiment was white as snow,
and the hair of his head like pure
wool;
his throne was fiery flames,
its wheels were burning fire."
(Dan. 7:9)

The "ancient of days" is an expression for the ancient one who has existed a great many years. The whiteness of his hair and his garment refers to the purity of God and the brightness of the realm of light. The throne is a judgment seat on a chariot. In biblical symbolism, fire and flame often accompany the appearance of God.

A fine hymn employing this figure is W.C. Doane's "Ancient of Days, who sittest throned in glory." Other verses refer to Father, Son, Holy Ghost and Triune God.

ners are two other circles enclosing the word *Pater* (Father) and the word *Filius* (Son). At the bottom angle is another circle with the words *Spiritus Sanctus* (Holy Spirit). Connecting the center circle with the others is a band inscribed *est* (is). The three outer circles are connected with each other by bands inscribed *non est* (is not). The shield may be read, "The Father is God," "The Father is not the Son," and so on around.

Triangles and Three-Fold Figures

The equilateral triangles alone or with a circle, the trefoil, the triquetra, three interwoven circles, three fishes in a triangle and other unified groupings of three are obvious symbols for the Trinity.

II. GOD THE FATHER

Ancient of Days

This phrase comes from the book of Daniel. "As I looked,
thrones were placed
and one that was ancient of days
took his seat;

Hand of God

This is the oldest symbol of God the Father. It is found in scenes of the Baptism of Christ where the hand of the Father reaches down from a cloud in blessing over the Son. In some cases two hands appear. By this symbol the power of God is emphasized. Usually the hand is accompanied by rays of light which are sometimes in the form of a three-rayed nimbus. See HAND in the Christmas-Epiphany section.

III. GOD THE SON, JESUS CHRIST

Cross

Because of his sacrificial death on the cross, this is the perfect symbol of Christ. It occurs in many different forms. The Latin cross, which is the form most often seen, symbolizes in addition the Passion of Christ. See CROSS in Holy Week section.

Cross and Serpent

"As Moses lifted up the serpent in the wilderness, so must the son of man be lifted up" (John 3:14). This verse together with the bronze serpent of Moses (Numbers 21:9) has led to the use of the cross with a serpent around it as a symbol of Christ and the Crucifixion. See also TAU CROSS in Advent section.

Fish.

Early Christians frequently used the fish as a symbol of Christ. The Greek word for fish (ICHTHUS in Roman letters) has five letters which are the initials of the Greek words meaning "Jesus Christ, God's Son, Savior."

Lamb

This symbol for Christ was often used in the Roman catacombs. It comes from John 1:29, where the words of John the Baptist are "Behold, the Lamb of God, (Latin *Agnus Dei*) who takes away the sin of the world!"

Rock

St. Paul wrote, "the Rock was Christ." (I Corinthians 10:4) He was referring to the rock which Moses struck in the wilderness to obtain water for the Israelites. (Numbers 20:11) St. Paul cites here a Jewish legend that this rock followed the Israelites in their travels. He implies that Christ pre-existed and cared for his people even before the Incarnation. Rocks in paintings can remind us of the Divine Presence.

Unicorn

Because of the legend about the unicorn's capture by a virgin and because he is hunted and slain by men, a medieval allegory made the unicorn a symbol of Christ. A Bible verse used in this connection is Luke 1:69, "God has raised up a horn of salvation for us in the house of his servant David." In Bible times the horn was symbolic of strength. The "horn of salvation" means a mighty savior.

Attributes of Christ used in art include globe with a cross (his sovereignty); the

five wounds of the Crucifixion; Greek letters such as alpha and omega (first and last), XP (chi and rho—first two letters of "Christ"), IHS ("Jesus"); a book, possibly with inscriptions. Three of the inscriptions are: *"Ego sum lux mundi"* (I am the light of the world, John 8:12), *"Ego sum resurrectio"* (I am the resurrection, John 11:25, *"Pax vobis"* (Peace be with you, John 20:19,26).

IV. HOLY SPIRIT (HOLY GHOST)
(See also under Pentecost.)

Dove

The most common symbol of the Spirit is taken from the account of Jesus' Baptism: a white dove with the three-rayed nimbus.

Eagle

In rare instances the eagle does duty as a symbol of the Holy Spirit. Irenaeus, in writing about the four living creatures, likens the eagle to "the Spirit hovering with his wings over the Church." The eagle is depicted on some old fonts. In some cases this may be intended to show that the eagle like the Spirit renews the life of the baptised Christian, just as according to legend this bird was supposed to renew its youth by flying near the sun and then plunging into water. More common symbolic uses of the EAGLE are found in the Easter section.

Fire or Flames

This symbol of the Spirit comes from the account of the first Christian Pentecost when tongues of fire descended on the disciples (Acts 2:3).

Sanctifier of the Faithful

This phrase, descriptive of part of the work of the Spirit, is found at the beginning of the Great Litany of the Book of Common Prayer. "Sanctify" comes from a Latin word meaning to make holy.

"Come Holy Ghost, our souls inspire" is the translation of an old Latin hymn. In symbolic language it tells of the gifts of the Spirit.

The Transfiguration, August 6

This festival commemorates the event chronicled in the first three gospels (Matthew 17:1-8; Mark 9:2-8; Luke 9:28-36), when Jesus took three chosen disciples, Peter, James and John, to a mountain top to pray. As the three watched on the mountain Jesus' face became radiant with a supernatural light, and Moses and Elijah seemed to be talking with him. Peter wanted to put up three tentlike shelters (tabernacles or booths) for them. Overcome with awe, the disciples heard a divine voice coming out of a cloud, "This is my beloved Son; listen to him" (Mark 9:7).

The prophet Elijah, who was expected to reappear just before the Messiah, is a messianic symbol, while Moses stands for the Jewish Law given to him in the form of the Ten Commandments on Mount Sinai (Exodus 31:18). The radiant light and the cloud signify God's presence.

Artists generally have pictured the mountain in a symbolic way as a low mound upholding Jesus, Elijah and Moses, while the three disciples appear below in the foreground. *Three tabernacles* (tents) serve as a symbol for the event. Another symbol used consists of a *crown* enclosed in *rays of glory* representing Christ the King of Glory.

A very appropriate symbol found in Raphael's painting of the Transfiguration is a cloud of light surrounding Christ. This can be depicted by the use of the figure of Christ or a cross to represent him with an *aureole around the figure*. An aureole is a field of radiance and light enclosing a body. It is a symbol of divinity.

Holy Cross Day, September 14

Another name for this day is the Exaltation of the Holy Cross. In legend the day is irrevocably connected with St. Helena, the mother of the Roman Emperor Constantine. She is said to have found the wood of the true cross at Golgotha in the early fourth century. Constantine erected a Church of the Holy Sepulcher at the spot and it was consecrated on September 13, 335.

Crosses of various kinds seem appropriate to this day. The principal types of crosses are the tau cross, with three branches, the Latin cross with four parts of which the lower element or staff is about twice as long as the others, and the Greek cross with four equal branches. There are many variations of these elemental forms. One often seen is a Latin cross with a circle around the crossing, called the Celtic cross. A cross with the clothed figure of Christ the King is also appropriate. See CROSS in the Holy Week section.

All Saints, November 1

All Saints' Day is one of the major festivals of the year. The word "saint" in this designation is used in the scriptural sense of anyone who is a faithful believer. So this feast serves as a commemoration of all God's "servants departed this life in thy faith and fear."

A combination symbol of the *cross and crown* serves well for this day since it is a sign of the Christian's victory at death. In Revelation 2:10 John says, "Be faithful  unto death, and I will give you the crown of life." Another symbol of victory and triumph, which occurs in the catacombs, is the *palm leaf.* The palm leaves were sometimes combined with the monogram. Again we turn to Revelation (7:9) for this symbol: "Behold, a great multitude . . . standing before the Lamb, clothed in white robes, with palm branches in their hands." Still another figure for this day is the *hand of God* pointing downward with thumb and two fingers extended, surrounded by rays. This reminds us that "the souls of the righteous are in the hand of God, and no torment will ever touch them." (Wisdom of Solomon 3:1).

Appendix

Games With Symbols

For individuals or teams several games may be based on symbols.

(1) *Identifying and explaining symbols.* For this use either drawings of symbols or a word (such as "crown") spoken or written. The object is to tell in what connection the symbol usually appears and briefly what it means.

(2) *Picking symbols out of a picture.* How many can you identify and list in a particular picture?

(3) *Bible verses.* Make a list of Bible verses relating to a certain group of symbols and see how many symbols can be identified by reading the verses. Many suitable verses are given in this book.

(4) *Treasure hunt.* Visit a church which has a considerable number of symbols in stained glass, carvings, or decoration and see how many can be found. Alternatively, a leader may give a list of symbols known to be found there and see who can find them all first. Similar games might be based on a certain room in a museum.

Making Seasonal Scenes

Symbolic scenes or posters may be desired for decorative purposes or bulletin covers. In addition to individual symbols the following may be suggestive.

Advent

The Advent wreath with candles or a corona (crown-shaped) candle holder with candles makes an appropriate scene to illustrate the season. More elaborate would be a Jesse tree. A Messianic symbol of Christ for Advent is the Sun of Righteousness. This is made up of an IHC or IHS in a circle which is surrounded by rays of glory, alternating straight and wavy.

Christmas

As a substitute for the Christmas crèche scene a triptych could be made to represent (1) Annunciation, (2) Nativity, (3) Shepherds, by using (1) lily in vase or fleur-de-lis, (2) manger with crossed legs at each end, monogram IHS above optional, (3) shepherd's crooks.

Epiphany

A triptych for the Visit of the Magi: (1) Star with rays including one long ray pointing to earth; (2) manger with crossed legs in a shed and a Christ symbol above the manger; (3) three crowns; or three caskets; or small chest (gold), cornucopia (incense) and ciborium (myrrh).

For the Baptism of Christ (Epiphany season): Hand of God overhead, dove flying down, fish or dolphin with wavy lines below. Some Sundays-after-Epiphany subjects which may be used singly or combined for the season:

Baptism of Christ: A scallop shell with three drops of water below (representing the Trinity formula of Holy Baptism).

Call of Disciples: A boat with one mast, fisherman in it (as Christ), fish alongside as disciples; twelve stars or twelve sheep as disciples. A large Greek cross with three small ones in each of the four angles.

Healing Ministry: Laying on of hands (on the sick) or ampulla (cruse) of oil for anointing.

The Transfiguration: For a triptych, a scroll for Elijah on one side and tables of Law for Moses on the other side of a cross or a monogram of Christ in the middle; or a cross with the two symbols in upper angles and three tents below (middle tent at base of cross). Another idea: two tablets of the Law for Moses with a flaming chariot wheel superimposed on them and a monogram of Christ above. See also Transfiguration in FEASTS OF THE PENTECOST SEASON.

Lent

A large Latin cross with an angel in each upper quarter and in the lower quarters, on the ground, a fox (see entry under DEVIL in Lent section) on one side and on the other a raven. This bird represents God's care for a desert saint, originating from the story of Elijah in the wilderness fed by ravens (I Kings 17:4). The same bird is also an attribute of the desert saints, Paul the Hermit and Anthony of Egypt, who were fed daily in their desert solitude by a raven bringing them bread.

A medieval custom for mid-Lent suggests a scene based on the four evangelists. In the medieval ceremony the four gospel books (Matthew, Mark, Luke, John) were placed at the four corners of the altar by deacons preparatory to an instruction by the priest on the four evangelists' symbols. Following out this idea in a scene, the four deacons could be represented as the evangelists at the corners of the altar with their symbols shown on them, or more simply four books with such symbols. For Matthew a winged man; for Mark a winged lion; for Luke a winged ox; for John an eagle.

A device appropriate to Lent is the Jerusalem cross which is also called the crusaders' cross. It appeared on the coat of arms of Godfrey of Bouillon, the first Latin king of Jerusalem (1099). The device condists of a large Greek cross with a smaller Greek cross placed in each of the four angles. This should be red crosses on a white background.

Palm Sunday

This may be represented by crossed palm branches and in the center above them the orb and cross symbolizing the triumph of Jesus Christ.

Holy Week or Good Friday

A square or upright rectangle divided into four parts by a cross. Some of the instruments of the Passion are shown in each of the four areas, but related to a particular time such as the scourging, Christ crucified, or the deposition.

Another scene: The crucifixion cross with darkened sun (shown with rays) and moon above, one in each corner, I.N.R.I. on board on the top cross arm, crown of thorns at the crossing, perhaps serpent or skull at the base (or some of the Instruments of the Passion such as nails and pincers).

An arrangement of the Instruments of the Passion.

Easter

An appropriate scene for the Good Friday to Easter period is Jonah and the Whale. This may be made of cardboard and construction paper including boat with mast and sail, figure of Jonah, whale in a blue sea (with whale's mouth large enough to accommodate Jonah). Jonah appears in the boat from Palm Sunday to Maundy Thursday, in the whale on Good Friday and Easter Eve, emerging from the whale for Easter Day and Week.

An ancient arrangement of peacocks, a resurrection symbol, places a pair of them, one on each side of a chalice or vase from which they are about to drink. A cross over the chalice may be added.

A triptych or series of scenes for Easter Day can be made out of the lessons used on Holy Saturday. The three essential Bible incidents to be symbolized are the story of Creation (Genesis 1:1-2:2), Israel's deliverance from Pharaoh at the Red Sea (Exodus 14:10-15:1) and the Resurrection of Christ. Since light in darkness, typified by the lighting of the paschal candle, is a symbol of God and of Jesus Christ, the Creation story can be shown by the sun and moon with God's hand between them. Two walls of water, designated by wavy lines, with stick figures in between can serve for the Red Sea incident. The cross over an open stone coffin or some other Easter symbol can indicate the Resurrection. Two further scenes are appropriate. After Creation came the flood (Genesis 7) which is usually pictured by Noah's ark. God's presence at the Exodus appears in a pillar of cloud by day and a pillar of fire by night to guide the Israelites on their journey (Exodus 13:21). See Easter Vigil service in the Proposed Book of Common Prayer.

John Mason Neale translated an ancient Greek Easter hymn, "Come, ye faithful, raise the strain," of which the first stanza reminds us of the connection of the Exodus with Easter.

Come, ye faithful, raise the strain

Of triumphant gladness;
God hath brought his Israel
Into joy from sadness;
Loosed from Pharaoh's bitter yoke
Jacob's sons and daughters;
Led them with un-moistened foot
Through the Red Sea waters.

Pentecost

A fan of red and yellow (or two shades of red) tongues of flame makes a showy Pentecost scene. Remember to use seven tongues of fire. Another pictorial symbol can represent the seven gifts of the Holy Spirit by using either seven doves or a seven-branched candlestick with flaming candles. The seven gifts are wisdom, understanding, counsel, might, knowledge, holy fear of the Lord, true godliness. The sevenfold gifts are based on Isaiah 11:2 in the Septuagint (Greek) version. The seventh is not found in English versions.

Suggestion for colors: Use collage of colored construction papers, colored carbons for spirit duplicators, ball point or felt tipped pens of different inks, poster paints for large scenes.

Index of Entries

Index of Bible References

Bibliography

Index of Entries

Index of Bible References

BIBLIOGRAPHY

Days and Seasons

Cowie, Leonard W. and Gummer, John Selwyn, *The Christian Calendar*, Springfield, Massachusetts: G. & C. Merriam Company, 1974.

McArthur, A. Allan, *The Evolution of the Christian Year*, London: Student Christian Movement Press, 1953.

Shepherd, Massey H., Jr., *The Oxford American Prayer Book Commentary*, New York: Oxford University Press, 1950.

Biblical

Buttrick, George A., ed., *The Interpreter's Dictionary of the Bible*, (4 vol.), New York: Abingdon Press, 1962.

Hastings, James, *Dictionary of the Bible*, revised ed., Frederick C. Grant and H. H. Rowley, eds., New York: Charles Scribner's Sons, 1963.

James, M. R., *The Apocryphal New Testament*, Oxford: The Clarendon Press, 1924.

Symbolism

Appleton, Leroy H. and Bridges, Stephen, *Symbolism in Liturgical Art*, New York: Charles Scribner's Sons, 1959.

Ferguson, George W., *Signs and Symbols in Christian Art*, New York: University Press, 1954.

Reau, Louis, *Iconographie de l'Art Chretien*, (3 vols.), Paris: Presses Universitaires de France, 1955-1959. (Volume 2, *Iconographie de la Bible*, is especially helpful.)

Webber, F. R., *Church Symbolism*, Cleveland: J. H. Jansen, 1927.

Art and Literature

Jacobus de Voraigne, *The Golden Legend*, trans. Granger Ryan and Helmut Ripperger, London and New York: Longmans, Green & Co., 1941.

Jameson, Anna, *Legends of the Madonna*, revised ed., Estelle M. Hurll, ed., Boston: Houghton Mifflin Company, 1896.

_____, *Sacred and Legendary Art*, revised ed., Estelle M. Hurll, ed., Boston: Houghton Mifflin Company, 1896.

Male, Emile, *The Gothic Image: Religious Art in France of the Thirteenth Century*, trans. Dora Nussey, New York: Harper and Row, Publishers, 1958.

White, T. H., trans. & ed., *The Bestiary: A Book of Beasts*, New York: G. P. Putnam's Sons, 1954.